"When Deidra first told me about this book, I heard in her voice the heart and hope behind her work. I heard the struggle inherent in writing, researching, and attempting to live the core principles you'll find in these pages. I also heard steady hope and faith. *One: Unity in a Divided World* is a moving and thoughtful critique of the status of oneness, restoration, reconciliation, and grace in America. This book will challenge, excite, transform, and inspire everyone who dreams of an end to division and polarization—in the Church, in our communities, in the workplace, in our homes, and in our very own souls."

—John Perkins, cofounder, Christian Community Development Association; founder, John and Vera Mae Perkins Foundation for Reconciliation, Justice and Christian Community Development; author of *Dream with Me*

"*One: Unity in a Divided World* is not only a timely book for today's Church, but it's also desperately needed. We emerge from the wreckage of 'culture wars' and church splits broken and scarred. Prejudice and privilege have damaged us, relational dysfunction and division have seared our souls. We stand separated, alone. Yet Deidra dares to walk among the wreckage, uncovering truths, rediscovering words like *reconciliation, forgiveness, oneness, unity*. Tenaciously and tenderly she reminds us of an identity and calling lost and forgotten. If you're searching for tools to help you rebuild unity in today's divided world, learn from Deidra. She's a wise, humble, and hope-filled guide."

—Jo Saxton, speaker and author; board chair of 3D Movements

"In *One: Unity in a Divided World*, Deidra points us toward change in our hearts. Unity must begin with each one of us before we can transform the Church. We the people must change! This is a timely book that will break through the ethnocentrism we have allowed to dictate our hearts and churches. The process toward reconciliation will begin in our hearts and communities first. *One* brings hope and healing to a divided and broken people. I highly recommend it to those seeking to understand the first and next steps toward racial unity."

—Tasha Morrison, founder of Be the Bridge

ONE

ONE

Unity in a Divided World

Deidra Riggs

BakerBooks

a division of Baker Publishing Group
Grand Rapids, Michigan

© 2017 by Deidra Riggs

Published by Baker Books
a division of Baker Publishing Group
P.O. Box 6287, Grand Rapids, MI 49516-6287
www.bakerbooks.com

Printed in the United States of America

Library of Congress Cataloging-in-Publication Data
Names: Riggs, Deidra, 1964– author.
Title: One : unity in a divided world / Deidra Riggs.
Description: Grand Rapids : Baker Books, 2017. | Includes bibliographical
    references and index.
Identifiers: LCCN 2016045290 | ISBN 9780801018435 (pbk. : alk. paper)
Subjects: LCSH: Church—Unity.
Classification: LCC BV601.5 .R54 2017 | DDC 262.001/1—dc23
LC record available at https://lccn.loc.gov/2016045290

Unless otherwise indicated, Scripture quotations are from the Holy Bible, New International Version®. NIV®. Copyright © 1973, 1978, 1984, 2011 by Biblica, Inc.™ Used by permission of Zondervan. All rights reserved worldwide. www.zondervan.com

Scripture quotations labeled Message are from THE MESSAGE. Copyright © by Eugene H. Peterson 1993, 1994, 1995, 1996, 2000, 2001, 2002. Used by permission of NavPress. All rights reserved. Represented by Tyndale House Publishers, Inc.

Scripture quotations labeled NKJV are from the New King James Version®. Copyright © 1982 by Thomas Nelson, Inc. Used by permission. All rights reserved.

Scripture quotations labeled NLT are from the *Holy Bible*, New Living Translation, copyright © 1996, 2004, 2015 by Tyndale House Foundation. Used by permission of Tyndale House Publishers, Inc., Carol Stream, Illinois 60188. All rights reserved.

Scripture quotations labeled Weymouth are taken from the 1912 Weymouth New Testament, no copyright information—public domain.

Some names and details have been changed to protect the privacy of the individuals involved.

17 18 19 20 21 22 23   7 6 5 4 3 2 1

In keeping with biblical principles of creation stewardship, Baker Publishing Group advocates the responsible use of our natural resources. As a member of the Green Press Initiative, our company uses recycled paper when possible. The text paper of this book is composed in part of post-consumer waste.

For Mom and Dad

So Much Love

A Great Need

Out
Of a great need
We are all holding hands
And climbing.
Not loving is a letting go.
Listen,
The terrain around here
Is
Far too
Dangerous
For
That.

By Hafiz

CONTENTS

INTRODUCTION

The only reason I knew I'd hurt Steven's feelings is because he told me so. One afternoon, in a room at the church we both attended, Steven and I sat face-to-face, a table between us. I remember it like it was yesterday. He had asked if we could talk.

"Something you said to me really hurt my feelings," he'd said to me during a phone call. "Can we talk about it?"

I was completely caught off guard. I racked my brain trying to remember everything I'd ever said to this man I'd known for just a few weeks. My husband, Harry, was the new pastor of this church and I, the new pastor's wife, had already stumbled into my first altercation. Steven had become a fast friend to my husband and me. He greeted us warmly each Sunday in a comfortable way that made us feel welcomed. He did not put on airs. He did not try too hard. He liked cigarettes and beer and was doing his best as a single dad to raise his son. We liked Steven and were grateful for his friendship.

So when Steven told me I'd offended him, my heart sank. "Of course we can meet," I told him. We checked our calendars and found a day that worked well for both of us. The fixer in me was frustrated that we couldn't just go ahead and get it over with right there on the phone, but I knew it would be best to meet face-to-face. That was important to Steven, and to me too.

Confrontation is a sticking point for many of us. Upon reaching an impasse with someone in our family, workplace, neighborhood, or church, we'd much rather avoid the situation than confront it. It feels easier to sweep the event under the rug or press it down inside of us. At face value, these seem like the less painful options. In some cases, we truly are able to release our hurt or disappointment without holding a grudge or letting it drive a wedge between us and the other person. Sometimes we really can work it out between us and God. From time to time we do find healing without ever needing to mention the discord to the other person.

More often than not, however, the thing just won't let us go. Each time we see that person or think of them, the impasse rises up to meet us. My body often tells me when I've let a situation get the best of me. I feel a tightness in my chest and a flush comes over my body. A pit opens up in my gut. My mind seems to ramp up a notch, as if it's preparing for a war of wits. Here's how I used to deal with people who got on my bad side: I put them on a mental list and made them work really hard to get off it. That was my go-to reaction. It was the wrong reaction.

Long before I spoke the words that offended Steven, God had begun to show me a new way of responding to people whose words or actions caused me pain. Using the teachings of Jesus found in Matthew 18, God began showing me how to respond when my feelings get hurt. What I learned is that when someone offends another person, God's way of responding is counterintuitive. God tells us to go directly to that person and let them know. "Work it out between the two of you," Jesus says to us (Matt. 18:15 Message). This passage is dealing specifically with sin in the body of Christ, but God has shown me the same principle applies when dealing with misunderstandings too. Jesus raises two important points in one short verse. First, he instructs us to go to that person and tell them what they've done. Second, we are admonished to keep it just between the two of us. Don't broadcast the disagreement. Don't shine a spotlight on the situation for all to see. Go quietly, with humility and respect, and face the offense together.

As I began to understand what God was showing me in Matthew 18, I slowly started to see confrontation as a gift God extends to us. God desires oneness and unity for us. When we hold grudges and add people to our unappealing short lists, we invite division and disunity. One way to stop discord in its tracks is to bring it out into the open, set it down on the table between you and the other person, and talk about it face-to-face. After all, the word *confront* means to "bring face-to-face."[1] We can take courses, read books, and listen to podcasts, which give us specific techniques for dealing with confrontation, but I've found the very best instruction right in the pages of God's Word. When we come to the table to talk face-to-face with someone who has offended us, or someone we have offended, these are the two very best things we can do: (1) be filled with the Holy Spirit, and (2) embrace the truth of the famous love chapter, which tells us love "is full of trust, full of hope" (1 Cor. 13:7 Weymouth).

Love Hopes the Best

Some would say we've gotten too generous with love. They say too much talk about love waters down the gospel. I would caution us to reconsider. The good news of Jesus Christ is deeply rooted in love. However, the love we're talking about here is not weak or scripted. When we try to minimize the love-to-gospel ratio, we are treading on dangerous turf. I would argue that what we've watered down is not the gospel, but our understanding of love in the kingdom of God. This love transcends patriotism, ethnocentricity, language, belief, and even reciprocity. Consider the example of Christ who, in a supreme demonstration of God's love for us, died in our place *while we were yet sinners*. The love God calls us to is greater than life. To love like this is to live in such a way that, should we ever be faced with the choice, we too would pay with our lives as a demonstration of our love.

The gospel of Jesus Christ is God's love letter to his creation. We can no more water it down than we can convince God to stop loving us. We proclaim, along with Paul: "Christ's love compels us" (1 Cor. 5:14).

By the time Steven asked me if we could talk, I'd had many opportunities to test this theory of confrontation from Matthew 18 and find that it is true. Going straight to a person who has hurt me (and to that person only), filled with the Holy Spirit and full of trust and hope, is always better than the alternative. The alternative is to talk badly about that person to anyone who will listen. The alternative is to practice snarky speeches I will recite to that person the next time we meet. The alternative is to let my hurt seethe and roil beneath the surface until it morphs into anger and, inevitably, hatred.

I later learned that Steven *had* gone to someone else before he came to me. He told me he had talked to his grandmother and told her I'd said something that had hurt his feelings. And do you know what Steven's grandmother did? She told him about Matthew 18. Then she told him he needed to talk with me face-to-face!

Sitting across from one another at a table, Steven and I each had our hopes solidly anchored in the words of Matthew 18 and confronted the issue at hand. Yes, it was awkward at first. He wanted to say what he had to say just right. I wanted him to know I was not his enemy. As the conversation progressed, it was clear that following God's process was worth it. Our conversation remained calm. No one yelled or acted defensively. I apologized. We prayed together.

If Steven had not confronted me, I never would have known I had hurt him. I probably would have kept on offending him and, over time, our friendship would have fallen apart. We would have avoided each other at church on Sundays, walking down opposite aisles and timing our arrivals so we wouldn't have to converse. I would have shrugged it off, blaming Steven for the rift between us, never realizing I'd been complicit in our friendship's demise. It doesn't matter that I never intended to hurt Steven. What matters is that he was hurt—and because of something I'd said. We found our way to that table through the power of the Holy Spirit. And thankfully, we came out remaining friends.

Later, when I began experiencing anxiety attacks (unrelated to my talk with Steven) that made it difficult for me to attend church, Steven and I sat together in the balcony for the service every Sunday. Our confrontation laid the foundation for a solid friendship. To this day, Harry and I both hold Steven in high esteem. God blessed our friendship. He reconciled us—through a face-to-face conversation at an ordinary table on a typical afternoon.

God's Invitation

I wrote this book because I think God has extended this same invitation to us. I believe God is inviting us to sit down face-to-face and deal with some of the stuff that keeps driving us further and further apart from one another.

Authors joke about giving birth to a book. We speak wryly about how writing a book is like cutting our wrists and bleeding out onto the page. We chuckle about excavating words, sentences, paragraphs, and chapters from somewhere within us we didn't know existed. Only, we are not joking. And there is no epidural for this.

Bringing new life into the world is risky business. The creative process requires a reckoning of heart, mind, body, and soul. We know our readers want us to get to the crux of the matter in a way that offers a tangibly satisfying answer to the question, "Who cares?"

The honest truth is that the words in this book scared me. I did not want to be the messenger of them. To do so meant I'd have to take my ideologies, experiences, preferences, and comfortable places and offer them up to God for examination. To explore the truth of what it means to be one and to work toward unity, I'd have to confront the schisms and divisions I've harbored in my heart and rationalized as justified. In other words, I'd have to come clean.

All of this was going on inside of me—all without my knowledge. I was afraid of the book, but I didn't know I was afraid. All I knew was that I was stuck. I could not write. Not a single word beyond the twenty thousand I had already written. With my deadline quickly approaching, I became a wrecking ball to anyone who dared ask how the book was coming along. I shut down, and I shut people out. The less I wrote, the less I was able to write. I asked for an extension on my deadline. I scrapped the twenty thousand words I had. I cried. I stared into space. I prayed. Still, nothing.

Then one evening, while I was at a retreat, feeling as if all hope was lost, a gentle and kind woman walked up to me and said, "I really don't want to do this, but I think God wants me to pray for you." I had no leverage. I was out of options. So I told this sweet woman yes, and she prayed that I wouldn't be afraid of the book. I don't know how she knew I was afraid, but I needed that prayer. Her prayer seemed to come easily to her. It was not judgmental. She prayed like someone who was acquainted with prayer, but maybe not so much with walking up to someone and telling them they think God is asking them to pray for you. She was not showy or fancy. She was simply doing what she felt God was asking her to do. And her prayer broke me open.

I left her and wrote throughout that entire night and into the morning, without sleep. I wrote past the fear. I wrote out my biases and my prejudices so I could get to the crux of the matter—because that is the point, after all.

I wrote the bulk of this book longhand, in one of those Moleskine journals. The kind with a black cover and an elastic band. The elastic band wraps around the edge of the book when no one is writing in it, to keep it closed.

This book is a product of my body, and I don't say that to be dramatic. It began inside of my brown, wide-hipped female body. It made its way onto the page through my cramped fingers—fingers that wrapped around a pen for hours each day. Together, the Messenger of this book, the prayers and good cheer of the faithful, and the physical work of my hands coaxed these words out from the places they'd been hiding and into the light.

When I wrote the very last word of the last chapter of this book, I rose to my feet on the deck at the back of our home. My spine and rib cage, elbows and knees unhinged and unfolded. My muscles and tendons and ligaments lengthened. As I rose, I became aware of an ache, deep in the hollow of my left hip, in the space where the joint rests. I stood in the sun, the heel of my left hand pressing hard against the soft curve of my womanly hip, and I wondered why it hurt. The ache had not been there when that woman prayed for me that night. It had not been there when I began writing this book. But here it was, settling down into the depths of my left hip. When I moved to take my first step after writing that last word, I discovered a limp that had not been there before.

Slowly, like a Monarch butterfly on a lazy day in June, a single word floated across the fence of my backyard and marked a circuitous route to my consciousness. Solid and profound, it slipped between hand and hip and gave a name to the pain. "Jacob" was the one-word reminder, and I had to catch my breath. Indeed. I had wrestled my way with God through every black mark on each white page of this book that has found its way to you.

I imagine if you're reading this that you bring your own struggle to the page. I imagine you're walking with a limp of your own, or you are headed in that direction. Maybe you are out of breath from all the back and forth you've been doing with God about whatever it is that made you pick up this book. I suspect there are some schisms and divisions in your own soul that you've got to contend with before God.

You are welcome here.

A friend called the words on these pages a "treatise on oneness and unity." I had to open my dictionary to discover whether treatise is a good thing or a bad thing. Ultimately, however, that will be for you to decide. Here's what I'd like to suggest, if I may. I think it will help to bring your whole self to this book. Bring your body, your mind, your heart, and your soul. Bring your biases and your prejudices. Bring your hopes and your dreams. And bring your fears. Bring what makes you angry, along with the experiences that heal you. I've written some questions at the end of the book, should you feel an invitation from somewhere in your soul to venture a few steps further into the content of each chapter. Use the additional study for your personal growth or together with a group of trusted friends.

These are not hard words. At least not in my estimation. But they might just change something deep inside you as you work your way to the very last page. I pray these words gently bring us face-to-face with some of the hard truths about ourselves. I pray God's grace will transform us. I trust God's mercy to bring us to the very last word on the very last page of this book as people surrendered to the process of being reconciled first to God and then to ourselves, so we may finally be fully reconciled to others—even those we now call our "enemy."

These are the dreams I have for us. I feel like that gentle and kind woman who prayed for me that night. I'm tucking my dreams into the prayer Jesus prayed for all of us on the night he was betrayed. "I pray that they will all be one," Jesus said, "just as you and I are one—as you are in me, Father, and I am in you. And may they be in us *so that the world will believe you sent me*" (John 17:21, emphasis mine).

Oneness is God's desire for us. Unity is what Jesus prayed for us. The odds are definitely in our favor.

One afternoon I was reading a chapter in a beautiful book when a few words rose up from somewhere within me, like a poem. I scrambled to find my Moleskine journal so I could write down the words before they drifted away. Slipping that elastic band off the edge of the book, I scribbled the words in green marker onto one of the few remaining blank pages in the journal:

> *When I die, I want to be wide open.*
> *I don't want to be tight-fisted, holding on*
> *to grudges or regrets. I don't want to*
> *have my back up because I'm still*
> *defending the walls I've built and*
> *the trenches I've dug and the invisible*
> *lines I've drawn.*
> *When I die, I want to go wide open.*

I hope this book breaks us wide open, to receive God's gift of oneness, unity, and reconciliation—in the trenches of life, yes, but also at ordinary tables, on typical afternoons.

ONE

A SOUL THAT HEARS WELL

The purpose is not to defeat your enemy, but to defeat the force that makes you hate each other. —Michelle Higgins

When my husband, Harry, was young, maybe three or four years old, his mom took him to a child's birthday party. Another boy at the party was bigger than Harry and fairly tough looking, as preschoolers go, but just a few weeks older than him. We'll call him David.

When Harry showed up at the birthday party, David was holding a helium-filled balloon. Spying the balloon, Harry walked up to David, looked into David's eyes, and said, "I'm going to take your balloon."

After Harry laid down the gauntlet, professing his intent to separate David from his balloon, David stared down his nose at Harry and said to him, "I will beat you up if you take my balloon."

Needless to say, Harry didn't get the balloon. He later recounted the details of the incident to his wise mom, who listened closely to the story and, in that moment, decided the best way to handle the situation would be to set up a playdate for Harry and David. She contacted David's mom, arranged a day for them to get together, and the next thing anyone knew, Harry and David were becoming best friends.

Their friendship grew and their families became close. They traveled together and spent holidays together; they grieved together and celebrated together.

Then one day, when Harry and David were about ten or twelve years old, David became very sick. He spiked a high fever—high enough that David had to be hospitalized. After he arrived at the hospital, David fell into a coma and the doctors and nurses worked resolutely to restore his health. Harry's family gathered to offer support and, thankfully, David began to recover. On the day David awoke from his coma, he asked to see Harry.

Being just a young boy, Harry had been fairly oblivious to the details of David's illness. All he knew was his friend was sick, so when Harry's mom told him David was awake and wanted to see him, Harry didn't think twice. He got in the car so his parents could drive him to the hospital to sit with David.

All these years later—almost five decades!—Harry and David remain close friends.

When I hear a story like this, I start feeling all warm and fuzzy on the inside and think to myself, *I love a story that ends well like that.* It's easy for me to forget how one wise and seasoned mother positively impacted the trajectory of this story. When Harry and David met, both were focused only on having that balloon. Harry's mom, however, was focused on the relationship between the young boys.

Isn't that how it goes? As those two boys saw it, getting that balloon was most important. But there was just one balloon and that one balloon could not be divided. Only one boy could have it, and each assumed the balloon should belong to him. As David saw it, the balloon was his in the first place. But, as Harry saw it, the balloon was something he wanted, and Harry was used to getting what he wanted.

In her great wisdom, Harry's mom knew more was at stake than just a balloon. What mattered most was the relationship between these two boys, and the impact a friendship could have on them both.

What's at Stake

When I watch my brothers and sisters in the body of Christ argue with one another or hear of churches splitting up or notice a congregation or conference with little to no diversity, I have to wonder what's at stake. I wonder what it would take to set up a playdate of sorts so we could try to figure out what common ground might look like. I wonder what answers I might get if I started asking questions like, "What's at stake for you here? Why are you arguing so loudly and calling people names? Why can't we keep worshiping together? Why can't we figure out how to add some people of color (*or* some white people or some women or some fill-in-the-blank, depending on the situation) to the speaker lineup? What are we clinging to so tightly?"

What's "at stake" for you?

Despite our good intentions, passion for justice, or desire to "defend the gospel," we often let ourselves get in the way.

In his book *The Road to Character*, David Brooks emphasizes this tendency:

> The United States ambassador to the United Nations, Samantha Power, perceptively observes that some people put themselves "at stake" when they get involved in a cause. That is to say, they feel that their own reputation and their own identity are at stake when decisions are made. *They are active in the cause in part because of what it says about them, and they want their emotions and their identity and their pride to be validated along the way.*[1] (emphasis mine)

This question of identity is a crucial element in the journey toward the oneness Jesus desires for us. If we can extricate our identity from the result of any discussion, argument, debate, or conversation, we stand a much better chance of achieving the harmony we so richly desire. Our identity is not impacted by whether or not others agree with us, or even by what others think about us. Instead, finding the right perspective on *who we are* is based on understanding *whose we are*. If I can rest in the confidence of knowing that neither my reputation nor my identity is founded on whether I "win" a particular argument or choose the "right" side, my investment becomes less and less about proving you wrong and more about building a relationship with you. A relationship based not on the ways we differ but on the elements of our stories, personalities, and experiences that enrich, stretch, and refine each of us.

Of course, this doesn't mean our differences automatically disappear. They don't. Nor should they. All kinds of differences contribute to the beautiful fabric of God's creation. As we grow in relationship with one another, our differences become supporting players in the main act of what we are building together.

Passing Through

In a 2012 podcast, Krista Tippett interviewed Rabbi Jonathan Sacks, who said, "[We] are enlarged by the people who are different from us."[2]

This is a profound thought, and it calls each of us to invite God to broaden our horizons, expand our views, and stretch us by teaching us how to pass through the differences of those who journey with us—but not like us. What does it mean to *pass through our differences?* We pass through our differences by being fully present when we encounter them. With our full attention, we give praise to God for his creative work, made manifest in the unique makeup of each person we meet. We suspend judgment—and pray others do the same for us. We listen with our hearts and let our view of things take a breather. As Terry Tempest Williams writes, "Can we listen with our whole beings, not just our minds, and offer our attention rather than our opinions?"[3]

Either we lean into all of who the other person is, or we don't. Either we acknowledge, celebrate, and honor the differences between us or we ignore or disparage them and, by extension, cut short the potential for experiencing the fullness of the relationship—the depth of the friendship. Passing through our differences does not ignore or negate them. But passing through them, rather than pushing against them, lets us absorb and be absorbed by the things that make us different from one another. We pass through our differences again and again. This is not the same as wallowing in them until they become all we see. We pass through them in celebration and thanksgiving to God for his extravagant creativity and rich imagination. The direct result of passing through these differences is that we each stand as better, richer, more complete representations of God's image in the world. Passing through leads from the heart. The opposite is bracing against. Passing through our differences is an exercise in grace. Grace is essential to finding oneness.

An Understanding Heart

I often wonder how best to help us find our way to *oneness*, which is not the same as *sameness*. How can we help take the focus off our personal, metaphorical, helium-filled balloons and get us to collectively focus on what matters most of all?

I guess one step might be to identify the balloon, right? For some of us, the balloon might represent power, health, comfort, wealth, safety, or the conviction of being right or justified or vindicated. For others, the balloon might represent freedom, status, peace, or shelter—for ourselves or for others. Or maybe we're simply driven by the fact that all we've ever known is the importance of hanging on to our balloon. No matter what.

While Harry and David may have gotten distracted by that birthday balloon, let's be fair in our conversation here. Many of the disputes in our history have had, at their root, the question of who gets to claim ownership of something (or—when we're at our very worst—some*one*). One of the most intriguing accounts of this type of dispute is outlined in the Old Testament book of 1 Kings.

In that story, two prostitutes present themselves to King Solomon, asking him to resolve a dispute between them.

"Please, my lord," one of them began, "this woman and I live in the same house. I gave birth to a baby while she was with me in the house. Three days later this woman also had a baby. We were alone; there were only two of us in the house.

"But her baby died during the night when she rolled over on it. Then she got up in the night and took my son from beside me while I was asleep. She laid her dead child in my arms and took mine to sleep beside her. And in the morning when I tried to nurse my son, he was dead! But when I looked more closely in the morning light, I saw that it wasn't my son at all."

Then the other woman interrupted, "It certainly was your son, and the living child is mine."

"No," the first woman said, "the living child is mine, and the dead one is yours." And so they argued back and forth before the king.

Then the king said, "Let's get the facts straight. Both of you claim the living child is yours, and each says that the dead one belongs to the other. All right, bring me a sword." So a sword was brought to the king.

Then he said, "Cut the living child in two, and give half to one woman and half to the other!"

Then the woman who was the real mother of the living child, and who loved him very much, cried out, "Oh no, my lord! Give her the child—please do not kill him!"

But the other woman said, "All right, he will be neither yours nor mine; divide him between us!"

Then the king said, "Do not kill the child, but give him to the woman who wants him to live, for she is his mother!" (1 Kings 3:17–27 NLT)

The women who stood before the king were motivated by intense feelings of loss and fear, grief and shame, anger and pain. Imagine yourself in their place. At first, it may be tempting to jump to the defense of the woman whose child was alive and had been stolen in the night by the woman whose child had died. "How could anyone steal another woman's child?" we may be tempted to ask. But what must it be like to wake up and discover your child's lifeless body there beside you in the bed, and then to realize their life had slipped away while they lay sleeping, beneath your own body? How must that impact your sense of reality? It was a tragic situation, to be sure, and the two women found themselves at an impasse. Blinded by their very real and legitimate anguish, these two women sought a solution in the court of the king.

This story has stood the test of time as an example of the great wisdom of this young king. Not long before these two women stood before him, desperate for a resolution, King Solomon had asked God for an understanding heart to lead his people, and God granted his request (see 1 Kings 3:9–12). Many translations of the Bible render the phrase *understanding heart* as wisdom, and that's not far from the truth. However, we get closer to the true meaning of Solomon's request when we return to the original language for the phrase "understanding heart": שָׁמַע לֵב, pronounced *shama' leb.*

Shama' means "to hear, listen to, obey." Maybe you're familiar with the Jewish prayer found in Deuteronomy 6, which begins, "Hear, O Israel: the LORD our God, the LORD is one" (v. 4). This prayer, called the Shema (based on this same Hebrew word for "hear") is a call to remember and revere the foundational truths of the Jewish faith. Solomon would have known this prayer. As he asked God for an understanding heart, Solomon may have been rooting his request in a deep-seated devotion and desire to honor the God of his fathers as he sought to rule fairly over God's people.

While *leb* means "heart," it refers to more than the organ with four chambers that pumps blood through our bodies. *Heart*, in this instance, means inner person, mind, will, understanding. In this instance, the word *heart* is closer in meaning to the word *soul*. And so, what King Solomon was really asking for from God was a soul that hears well; a soul that listens and then, based on what it hears, chooses the path that best honors God and serves others.

Looking at those two distraught mothers standing before him, King Solomon must have recalled his request for an understanding heart. Each woman had a lot at stake as they stood there, presenting their cases and awaiting his verdict. Like Harry's mother, who had to make a decision about how to deal with two boys who wanted the same balloon, King Solomon desired an outcome that would have a deeper impact than a simple decision *about* the baby. Solomon, as God's ambassador, was even more concerned about the heart of each woman who stood in his court, seeking justice. He was equally concerned about the heart of that child who would live his life under the import of Solomon's decision. Solomon's decision was *for* the baby. And Solomon's focus didn't stop there. His decision was also *for* the women. Both of the women.

Longing to Be Right

You and I might quickly look at two boys arguing over who gets to keep a birthday balloon or two distraught women seeking justice when only one baby is left between them, and try to figure out which one is "right." A longing to be right is often at the heart of our arguments, our divided churches, and our small social circles where everyone thinks and looks and lives exactly like us. We choose a side, and we fight for that side. When we do this, our focus is calibrated toward *about* rather than *for.*

What Solomon's and Harry's mothers knew is that being "right" isn't the goal. Jesus didn't say, "I have come that they may be right." It's easy to get confused. I know this, because I've done it. I've gotten mixed up and thought the whole reason Jesus came to earth, died on the cross, and then rose from the dead was to make sure I am always right (I'm sure my family members will gladly confirm this confusion that sometimes overtakes me). But what Jesus actually said was, "I have come that they may have life" (John 10:10). I know—"be right" and "have life" sound a lot alike. But let's be clear: it's life that Jesus came to give us. And not just any life. What Jesus came to offer us is *abundant life.*

When I do the math, the promise of abundant life carries more potential than a life in which I am always right. What a boorish lot that would make us all, if we were all always *right,* right? In fact, consider these thoughts from David Brooks:

> We are all sinners together. To be aware of sin is to feel intense sympathy toward others who sin. It is to be reminded that as the plight of sin is communal, so the solutions are communal. We fight sin together, as communities and families, fighting our own individual sins by helping others fight theirs.[4]

In Western culture, we are not so familiar with this communal perspective. We are individualists who often experience life with our needs and desires at the center of our focus. In contrast, cultures that foster a communal, or collective, perspective consider the group or the community to be of greater concern. I'm not here to say that one of these perspectives is correct and the other is not. My point is simply to present these two perspectives for our consideration. It's helpful to identify the perspective that best fits us as we think about how we work our way to the other side of our divisions—as individuals and as communities. Of course, whether we resonate more with an individualistic or a collective perspective, God's invitation to abundant life doesn't excuse us from the weight and consequence of our sin. As David Brooks reminds us, "We are all sinners together." Miraculously, once we realize this, we also understand that a benefit of having access to God is being empowered by the Holy Spirit to focus on loving our neighbor, without being concerned about whether our neighbor is right.

How Do We Love Well?

So, if this is true, how does it change the way we live today, in this moment, with all of the people in this world who think, act, believe, and live differently than we do? How do we love God in a culture and context filled with people with whom we disagree?

Let's begin here: God loves us. He loves all of us. God loves women who've had abortions. God loves men who dress in drag. God loves people who kill unarmed black men in America. God loves terrorists. God loves people who cheat on their taxes. God loves people who shoot to kill in movie theaters and elementary schools and then turn the guns on themselves. God loves the man who cheats on his wife, and God loves the wife abandoned by that man. God loves the woman who sleeps with a married man. God loves the person who cheats on a final exam. God loves the mom who lies about her drug use. And God loves the son who falls in love with the boy next door.

It is precisely because God loves us that he chose to reconcile us to himself. William E. Pannell says it this way: "Love precedes reconciliation, as Paul argues in his Corinthian letter—it was the love of Christ that was the wellspring of all his actions."[5]

But love is hard. It's easier to draw a line in the sand and then determine who's on our side and who isn't. It's easier to try to decide who gets the balloon and who doesn't. It's the way we often operate, isn't it? The haves and the have-nots. The Democrats and the Republicans. The police and the unarmed black man. Straight people and gay people. The Jews and the Gentiles. The clean and the unclean. There is nothing new under the sun.

Whatever keeps me from loving my neighbor is in direct opposition to God's desire for my life and for the body of Christ. God desires oneness, but when I let something come between me and my neighbor, I am living the opposite of that desire. That's not to say we should all "just get over" our hurts and disappointments. This is a lifelong journey. We take steps forward, and we take steps backward. The goal, however, is to not give up hope. The goal is to invite God to continually make all things new—in our relationships and in our view of others; even our enemies. We are seekers trying to figure out a way to navigate this great tension between God's promise to us of abundant life and the reality of a world with limited resources and people who scare, confuse, and misunderstand us.

"For God so loved the world that he gave his one and only Son, that whoever believes in him shall not perish but have eternal life" (John 3:16). This verse is an old favorite, right? It doesn't matter if you've been in church all your life or if you've never set foot in a sanctuary. You've probably heard some version of this verse sometime during your life. You may even have it committed to memory or matched up to some melody in your mind. But what does it mean, really?

Eugene Peterson paraphrases that famous passage in this way:

> This is how much God loved the world: He gave his Son, his one and only Son. And this is why: so that no one need be destroyed; by believing in him, anyone can have a whole and lasting life. God didn't go to all the trouble of sending his Son merely to point an accusing finger, telling the world how bad it was. He came to help, to put the world right again. (John 3:16–17 Message)

Remember: God sent his Son as the culmination of his great plan to win us back to himself. Now, the Bible tells us that *we* have this ministry of reconciliation—of living at one with God, ourselves, and one another (see 2 Cor. 5:19). Paul calls us Christ's ambassadors, and these are our marching orders:

> God put the world square with himself through the Messiah, giving the world a fresh start by offering forgiveness of sins. God has given us the task of telling everyone what he is doing. We're Christ's representatives. God uses us to persuade men and women to *drop their differences* and enter into God's work of making things right between them. We're speaking for Christ himself now: Become friends with God; he's already a friend with you. (2 Cor. 5:18–20 Message, emphasis mine)

God is calling us to fill the role of the wise parent or the wise young king mediating a dispute between two distraught members of his community. As God's ambassadors, we are called to raise the level of discourse and bring healing to those who are hurting and who draw deep lines of division or build tall walls of separation. Parker J. Palmer, author and founder of the Center for Courage and Renewal, states it this way:

> Today we . . . need to find a Third Way. That does not mean making cheap compromises, as in, "I'll stop caring about the poor if you'll stop caring about more money for the military." Instead it means holding our differences in ways that open us to possibilities we never would have imagined if we had failed to hang in with each other.[6]

To live into the oneness Jesus desires for us, we must keep hanging in with one another.

We are called to courageously own up to the ways we've drawn our own lines and built our own walls. This is how we love well. When we get called on the carpet for our complicity in systems, perspectives, and practices that divide, we act like the humbled basketball player who gets caught traveling on the court: we raise our hand and 'fess up. "My bad," we say. We take the penalty. We make course corrections. We apologize. We lament. We recognize that, though we are called to elevate the conversation, we are not above the conversation or immune to our own prejudices. And when someone from the other team raises her hand and says, "My bad," we do not shout her down or shut her out. Always, always, always, oneness is our goal.

An understanding of the Third Way lies at the end of the road to personal reconciliation. We must be reconciled first to God, and to ourselves, before we can be reconciled to one another or be agents of reconciliation in the world. This personal reconciliation is at the heart of the Great Commandment, through which Jesus entreats us to love God and then love others as we love ourselves.[7] Slowly, as we grow in love for God and for ourselves, we also grow in our ability to direct attention away from the superficial distractions (distractions designed by our true enemy to keep us suspicious of one another) and toward the oneness Jesus prayed for us. Sometimes this ability is a function of being an adult who mediates a dispute between their child and another person's child. Other times the ability to see the Third Way is the result of the supernatural intervention of, and our surrender to, the Holy Spirit in our lives.

Time and Spirit

We are often the child at the birthday party and a playdate is the very last thing on our minds. Other times, we are deeply and sincerely wounded and grieved, blinded by our own distress and in need of someone who will help us find our way. In moments like these, time helps us grow and the Holy Spirit heals us. While we await the work of time and Spirit, we also wait for the right moment to extend the invitation to a conciliatory playdate. There's no need to force a playdate when the time just isn't right or we are simply not ready for it. The work of time and Spirit is also part of the journey toward oneness, prepping us and shoring us up for that moment of rolled-up sleeves, hard conversations, and the staggering work of forgiveness. Let time and Spirit do their jobs. Reap the benefits of their care and wisdom. Then, once their work has been fulfilled, the places in our souls that once sagged wide open and where our grief and distress threatened to erase our voice, our hope, and the embrace of our holy identity stands a bit taller.

The Myth of Scarcity

Our enemy wants us to believe there's not enough goodness to go around. Our enemy has us surveying the landscape for the most desirable plot of grass atop the most fertile soil. We drive a stake into the ground, tie a flag to that stake, gather our people to ourselves, and dig a trench around the whole shebang. It is a never-ending torrent of division and separation. It is the opposite of oneness and reconciliation. And it is built on a myth that has worked so well for so long that we have come to mistake it for the truth.

> The myth of scarcity tells the powerful to accumulate and take and dominate, to be driven by the fear of Not Enough and Never Enough. We make our decisions out of fear and anxiety that there isn't enough for us. These core beliefs can lead us to the treacheries of war and hunger, injustice and inequality. We must keep others down so we can stay on top. We stockpile money and food and comforts at the expense of one another and our own souls. Throughout Scripture, we can see the myth of scarcity's impact on—and even within—the nation of Israel. The prophets wrote and stood in bold criticism against the empire's myth of scarcity that built on the backs of the poor and oppressed.[8]

This belief that there is not enough to go around, not enough of God's blessing or favor or goodness, keeps us insulated and in our silos—our buildings, our doctrines, our programs, and our budgets. Meanwhile, the world is watching us as we stand on our islands with our backs turned outward and our shoulders hunched.

I've looked for some deep meaning in the word *one* Jesus used in his prayer in John 17. But everything I read points to a simple, uncomplicated meaning of the oneness Jesus was speaking of. The oneness Jesus referred to was, quite simply, one. Undivided.

Of course, a person could substitute the word *reconciled* for the word *one*.

I don't have this all figured out; I'm on the same journey you're on. I struggle with wanting what I want when I want it. I struggle with making sure my anger doesn't guide me when faced with injustice or naysayers or angry people who try to quiet me down. I have to work at not putting other people down so that, when compared to *my* version of them, I come out smelling like roses. I am like the early Christians who had hoped for a valiant warrior who would teach them to slay ten thousand men with one awesome flourish of the sword. I want to be the bloody victor. I want to be the winner, and I want the world to stand up and take notice.

But Jesus's strategy is subversive, to the extreme. According to Jesus, everything we think we know about winning has to do with losing. Everything we think we know about gaining has to do with letting go.

God went first. He emptied himself. He humbled himself. He gave up his life in our place. The entire story of the Bible—from Genesis through Revelation—is a story of reconciliation. This God keeps hanging in with us, and he's motivated by love. The work of reconciliation weaves together being reconciled to God, being reconciled to yourself, and being reconciled to those around you. By this, the world will know that Jesus was sent by God.

When I disparage my neighbor, when I justify my dislike of my sister in Christ, when I rationalize my acts of unkindness or injustice, I am guilty of sin. When I mock or shame or exclude or ridicule—and especially when I do it in the name of Christ—I am in the wrong. When I turn a deaf ear or a blind eye to those who are gasping for breath, and when I tell the woman caught in adultery that she deserves what she gets, I have wandered off the narrow path and need someone to point me back to the Third Way.

When I imagine the Third Way, it looks like a vast table or a gigantic wraparound porch. My friend John Blase, a poet and theologian, describes it like this:

> Everyone's here. . . . It was a late summer picnic, people were wearing shorts, and there were stop-traffic legs but also regular-old legs. Speaking of legs, there were all these vets whose legs had been stolen in combat, and their legs had all been returned, and they were running around chasing each other like boys while their dear mothers stood with tears in their eyes and hands on their hips saying *Now wouldja just look at that.* Suddenly I feared there would not be enough food for everyone, but a young Natalie Wood cleared her throat and eased me: *John, there's so much here. This is the everlasting.* All my family and friends were there, plus famous people I've followed over the years like Johnny and June Carter. Yet also people I wouldn't have necessarily chosen to invite. But when I saw their faces, I couldn't help but feel a gathering tenderness toward them, so I walked over and could not stop saying, *I'm so glad you're here.* One of them, an older man who took his life when I was a young preacher, said, *Me too.* It was then I began to weep because I realized I, too, was a guest. And with God as my witness, that was such a gorgeous thought for this first-born who usually tries to ensure everyone's having a good time at the party, but there in that next place, I saw we were all free at last to lay down every role, real or perceived, every burden great or small. Everyone was there, and it was like we were laved in the eternal light of talk after dinner.[9]

Reconciliation invites everyone to the table, the wraparound porch, the picnic on a summer afternoon. All of us, even those we wouldn't have necessarily chosen to invite. And isn't that the point? We are not in charge of the guest list. We are guests along with everyone else.

TWO

INTEGRATED EXPERIENCES

When I first started thinking about writing this book, I was sure I'd be writing about race in the Church in America. Anyone who knows me knows my passion for bridging the divide that still exists among our congregations on any given Sunday morning. I find it astounding that we continue to worship in black churches and white churches, Hispanic churches and Asian churches, and on and on. In 1968, soon after the death of Martin Luther King Jr., James Baldwin said, "You must consider that the fact that we have a black church is, first of all, an indictment of a Christian nation. There shouldn't be a black church."[1]

Just a few months before, in a sermon titled "Remaining Awake through a Great Revolution," Dr. King leveled an equally convicting criticism at the Church in America, saying, "We must face the sad fact that at eleven o'clock on Sunday morning when we stand to sing 'In Christ there is no East or West,' we stand in the most segregated hour of America."[2]

As members of the body of Christ, our language and cultural differences and our music and sermon length preferences seem like weak and empty reasons for separating ourselves from one another and thinking it's okay to do so. It's been decades since Dr. King pointed out that Sunday morning at eleven o'clock is the most segregated hour in America. Yet, as of this writing, those words still ring true. Why is that?

We have been numbed and dumbed to all the reasons for this division in our institutionalized churches. We think it's completely normal and acceptable, but I find it hard to believe God agrees with us.

Yes, diversity in the pews and on the platform is the norm in some churches, but they are the exception. Standing like icons of US history, our churches speak a blatant testimony to what some call the original sin of the American nation. Racism is woven into the very fiber of American existence and continues to pervade many of the systems, institutions, and thought patterns of the land.

But this conversation is not only about racism. What more can be said about racism? Racism is the manifestation of something deeper. All of our conversations, conferences, summits, essays, articles, books, lawsuits, interviews, news reports, and discussions around the Thanksgiving table (Lord, have mercy) have examined racism from every angle and through every theological lens. The point here is not to prove or disprove racism. We each see the news reports and interpret them as seems best to us, based on our own peculiar mix of faith, worldview, culture, context, joy, and sorrow. Readers of a lighter hue will hear the stories of darker brothers and sisters and will have to make their own decisions about their truth. Others, with darker skin tones or non-European heritage will observe the actions of their lighter brothers and sisters and will have to make their own decisions about their truth. Christ, have mercy on us all.

While this is not a book about only racism, I am going to talk about it a little bit. Because racism springs from somewhere, doesn't it? God has used this issue and its prominence in the Church (especially in the United States) to get my attention about the staggering issues that drive the deep divisions and extensive polarization within the body of Christ. Racism is one manifestation of our fallen condition and one of the ways we let disunity and division ruin our witness of God's power to heal a broken world. Racism is one example of humanity's predisposition toward destruction when left to its whims or manipulated by fear or by the classically cunning lie that one of us can take hold of power and become like God.

For example, changing demographics suggest that in the near future in America, white people will no longer represent the majority of the population. As this awareness has become more evident, there has been "a sustained rise in hate groups," according to Heidi Beirich, leader of The Intelligence Project at the Southern Poverty Law Center, a nonprofit anti-terrorism organization. Beirich says the main element propelling the rise in hate groups is the changing demographics in the United States and the election of this country's first black president. "Hatred of black people is the driving force for America's hate movement," says Beirich. "But, over the years, as you have seen a change in sort of the population of people of color here, you can add to that mix dislike of Latinos and immigrants, dislike of gay people and, very recently, we have seen a huge outburst by every kind of hate group against the Muslim community."[3]

As a woman of color, and especially as I am given the opportunity to minister in and to the white evangelical community, my challenge is always to make space for grace in every single encounter. When I walk into a church and see that I'm one of a very few persons (or the only person) of color in the entire building, I can choose my response to that situation. *I have to* choose my response. Many others make this same kind of choice every single day: women, members of the LGBTQ community, people of Muslim faith and heritage, immigrants. Often, for those in the majority culture, these are not choices that must be made on a regular basis. Could it be that not having to navigate these choices also points to the fact that many of us don't get out beyond our comfort zones often enough?

Beyond Comfortable Congregations

We often choose churches and faith communities that envelop us in the comfort of people who look like us, think like us, vote like us, and dream like us. While that's a soothing place to be, it also serves as a recipe for failure when it comes to equipping us to lovingly engage with people who are different from us. As a result, we fall into old ways of thinking about the people who aren't like us. These are thought patterns we hold, which simply have never been explored, challenged, and replaced with a viewpoint that honors God and the *imago Dei*—the image of God—in each of us, in this Year of Jubilee. Our homogeneous congregations don't provide us with any practical or relevant experiences for learning how to love the others in our world.

Because American society is built on systems that were born out of racialized notions of humanity, it's extremely difficult to transform a church that has historically been comprised of one race into a multicultural congregation. It's not impossible, but the cost of such change is great. Don't get me wrong here. Churches can begin to intentionally make church staff hires that reflect more diversity. They can incorporate worship songs in different languages and with different instrumentation. They can plant satellites in neighborhoods with a diverse demographic. Each of these approaches helps to move the conversation forward, but there is no way to overstate the cost of doing this kind of work. The work of integrating a church is often debilitating because of the way it exposes and uncovers layers of latent issues, thought patterns, and reticence.

To be clear, when I talk about integrating a church, I mean more than building a church that merely looks and sounds colorful on Sunday mornings. Often when I write about the racial divide among our churches, a reader will write to tell me about a particular person or family of color who attends their predominantly white church. The emails I receive are very similar. They begin by thanking me for opening the conversation about the ways our churches continue to be divided among racial lines. They go on to say they are blessed by the black (or Asian or Hispanic) family that attends their church. The people contacting me are beautiful people, with kind and sincere hearts. I believe them when they say they wish things could be different. I believe them when they express astonishment that racism still exists today, even in our churches. The readers typically close their emails by saying the people of color in their congregation really seem to be comfortable there. The writers express gratitude for the experience of worshiping and serving with people of color in their church.

A church with one, two, or even a handful of people from a different race or culture is not an integrated church. I once worked with a group of people who were experiencing a change in the neighborhood around their church. The church had been a white church for more than one hundred years. Now, as the neighborhood changed, the congregation began to see more people of color in the sanctuary on Sunday mornings. The white members of the church were warm and kind and welcomed these new attendees to the worship service. As the people of color became more comfortable in the church, the worship service began to be punctuated with hand-clapping during the singing and *Amen-ing* during the preaching.

One afternoon I was engaged in a conversation with an older, long-term member of the congregation. She had weathered many seasons of ups and downs at that church—the kinds of ups and downs that most churches face. This new change, however, with different people bringing their worship styles with them to church on Sunday mornings, was a big challenge for this kind woman, and she struggled to find her footing as the changes seemed to press in around her. I sensed her discomfort, and she confirmed it for me when she said, "Well, they visited here before they decided to join. They saw how we were, so why don't they just do things our way?"

The important thing here is not what she said, but why. When we can uncover the why behind these kinds of statements, we get at the heart of what causes us to be so divided. The woman in the story above, who was struggling to find a way to truly embrace the new people in her church, expresses so much of what we all face when our world begins to feel as if it's shrinking and *they* are getting the upper hand over *us.*

If the people of color in a majority white congregation, neighborhood, school, or conference feel as if the elements of the experience—the leadership, programming, language, imagery, scheduling, and even potluck meals—reflect their humanity *and* take their story into account, that organization might be on the right track. If we were to sit down and talk with the leaders and members of these communities, we would likely find a high value placed on ideologies of inclusivity and cultural competency.[4] Naturally, these kinds of organizations must keep evaluating, and reevaluating, always being careful not to settle in and risk the possibility of becoming complacent in their work toward unity. If, however, people in a group feel as if they have to code switch to be accepted and understood, while others can get away without code switching,[5] it would be wise to begin to explore why this may be. Code switching is not always an indication of discomfort. People often choose to switch between different languages or dialects because it's a comfortable form of expression. However, consistently feeling as if one must defer to the majority's preferred way of communicating in order to be accepted often becomes an unfair burden on individuals in minority groups. This is true even when the person in the minority group *in a particular situation* is usually in the majority in most of that person's other interactions.

This Is Where the Revolution Begins

I certainly haven't given up hope in the future of the Church in America. As the country finds its way through a few of the rough patches looming ahead (by responding positively to changing demographics, showing resilience with regard to the political landscape, recovering economically disenfranchised communities, advocating for the marginalized around the world, etc.), the Church in America can stand as an example of unity in a divided world. In fact, the more we work toward the unity for which we've been created, the more the Church can take the lead in this hard, healing work that the country now faces. The road to unity in the Church begins in the heart of each person who claims Jesus as Lord and Savior. Your heart is where the revolution begins. Long before we end our need to rationalize our racially divided churches, we must end our need to rationalize our racially (and otherwise) homogeneous dinner parties, PTO meetings, book clubs, playgroups, and ski trips.

As believers in reconciliation and advocates for restoration, change begins at home.

This is why, when people email me to tell me about the person of color who attends their church, I sometimes write back and say, "I wonder what [insert name of person they've written about] would say about what it's like to be a person of color at your church?" I don't always ask that question because I don't always feel as if I've earned the right to ask it. But here in this book, I'd like to ask you the question. If, as you've been reading these thoughts about race in the Church, you've thought about a person or a group of people in your own church whose race, culture, or ethnicity (and possibly even language) are different from the majority of the people who go there, have you asked them what it's like *for them* to be part of this particular congregation? Of course, you'll have to determine whether or not you've earned the right to ask that question of them.

Maybe it's not a church. Maybe it's the Muslim child at your son's school or on your daughter's basketball team. Perhaps it's the new family with two moms that moved into the empty house next door. It could be the co-worker who parks his SUV next to your Prius each day and sports a bumper sticker proclaiming his membership in a movement or a political party with which you strongly disagree.

In so many ways, when it comes to destroying walls of division, it's easier to begin out in the world. It's easier to write a book about it or give a speech than it is to actually work toward reconciliation in our own lives. It's also easier to criticize others for not working hard enough or using the right words or implementing the correct strategy or inviting the best people to the table. God has chosen, however, to change the world *out there* by starting with what's going on *in here*—in the heart, mind, and soul of each person who has chosen him. As much as I desire for the Church to stand as a beacon to a hurting world, I can't expect something of Church leaders that I'm not willing to work through in my own life and in my personal relationships with the individuals God has placed in my real, everyday world.

Making Everyone Part of My Vocabulary

The Bible reminds us we have a stake in making peace: "If it is possible, as far as it depends on you, live at peace with everyone" (Rom. 12:18). Paul's use of the word *everyone* is a reflection of his complete understanding of the teachings of Jesus. Jesus was all about the everyones of the world. He did not exempt anyone from his love, grace, mercy, or invitation to salvation. If we desire to emulate the ways of Jesus, we've got to make sure *everyone* is part of our vocabulary when we engage the world. In my neighborhood, a car often parks in front of the church a few blocks from my house. On the back bumper is a sticker that sums up the goal of those who would seek to be reconcilers: "God bless the whole world. No exceptions."

It is possible to reconcile with anyone. I truly believe that. But remember, reconciliation is a process that begins when two opposing parties come together for the purpose of peace. If both parties are not willing to participate, what is often achieved is forgiveness from one party, but not reconciliation. Reconciliation requires that forgiveness be not only offered but also sought. In the same manner, if you are the one offering a sincere apology, but you find yourself met with someone who is resistant to your offering and unwilling to forgive, you have not achieved reconciliation. You may have done your part in taking ownership of the way your actions hurt the other person, but that is not the same as reconciliation. In both of these instances, you may even achieve some semblance of peace, but even the presence of that kind of peace does not equal reconciliation.

As reconcilers, we are ambassadors of the kind of peace spoken of in Ephesians 2:14–18:

> For he himself is our peace, who has made the two groups one and has destroyed the barrier, the dividing wall of hostility, by setting aside in his flesh the law with its commands and regulations. His purpose was to create in himself one new humanity out of the two, thus making peace, and in one body to reconcile both of them to God through the cross, by which he put to death their hostility. He came and preached

peace to you who were far away and peace to those who were
near. For through him we both have access to the Father by
one Spirit.

This peace gets at the heart of the everyone-ness Jesus
promoted. Even though Jesus crossed all sorts of imaginary
lines in his life on this earth, the concept of getting along
with everyone is often lost in what appear to be the flashier
elements of the story. The kind of reconciliation for which
Jesus advocates is the most unbelievable miracle of them all.
Despite its flashiness, however, even the disciples missed its
full implications.

We get glimpses of it though. Take Pentecost, for example,
when the Holy Spirit showed up and preached the good news
to everyone in such a way that they were each able to hear and
understand in their own language. Then there was the vision
Peter had while praying on the roof of a friend's house. There
on the roof, the Spirit of God made it clear to Peter that he
should no longer consider anything unclean. As a result of this
encounter, Peter began to share the message of God's salvation
with the Gentiles. Then there was Philip, who, one afternoon
found himself in the company of an Ethiopian. Philip told
this man the story of Jesus and then baptized the Ethiopian
into the faith.

The apostle Paul worked to unpack this message—that the
good news was not only for the Jews. The good news, it turns
out, is for everyone. And Jesus himself is our peace. Jesus tore
down the dividing wall and made the two (Jews and Gentiles)
one. Jesus desires oneness for all of us in the body of Christ,
all the time. When the world looks at us, they shouldn't see
any way to get between us. But the enemy is clever, and he

knows our weak spots. Often we make it far too easy for him. It's been that way from the beginning. We are weaker when we're divided. When we're off by ourselves, separated from the rest of the body, the enemy convinces some of us to believe his lies. Then he spends a little bit of time with the rest of the group and makes us believe a different lie. The result, of course, is that we turn against one another instead of remembering who our true adversary is.

We behave predictably, even though we claim to follow an unpredictable God. We give our critics too much to work with.

We think in our hearts that we believe God loves everyone, but when push comes to shove (we encounter someone who advocates strongly for a cause we oppose, or we experience an injustice or a betrayal or an unspeakable horror at the hands of another human), we don't act accordingly. On the flip side of these experiences we say to ourselves, "That everyone-ness may be good for Jesus, but I'm not Jesus."

Up Front and Regular

Not too long ago, I spoke with a friend of mine. He and my husband were in seminary together. When this friend graduated, he served as the pastor of a multiracial congregation. When he arrived at the church, the congregation was 60 percent black and 40 percent white. My friend was the first African American pastor to serve at that church.

One morning I talked with my friend, who shared with me the highs and lows of serving that congregation. At the end of our conversation I asked him, "If you were to counsel someone who is passionate about the message of oneness and unity in the body of Christ, what two or three steps would you offer?"

My friend took a very deep breath, and then he sighed and said, "I don't know."

"Do you think it's impossible?" I asked.

"No," he answered quickly. "It is possible."

Then we talked a little bit more. We talked about music and worship style and the faces of leadership in the local church and in the Church. We talked about the importance of being intentional when it comes to engaging the work of reconciliation. All things I've explored before, with different people who have different perspectives and reach different conclusions about *what we should do*.

Just as our conversation was ending, my friend said to me, "You know, I think there is one thing I would say about how to move the goalpost closer to a sense of integration. We have to be open about what's going on. We are one, and we need to keep reminding each other of that."

In my heart, I felt a keen sense that this was the answer I'd been looking for as my friend and I had been talking. His point was that we need to keep the goal of unity and oneness an *up front and regular* part of how we go about our everyday lives. Up front and regular, indeed. At church, at home, at school, in the community, as we vote, as we cheer for our favorite sports team, as we advocate and demonstrate, as we pray, and as we serve. We need to remind one another, and we need to be reminded ourselves, that we are ambassadors of unity.

Up front and regular is a modern-day translation of God's encouragement to the people of Israel, found in the book of Deuteronomy. Deuteronomy tells the story of God working to teach the Israelites how to get along with one another as a new nation—a mixed multitude—that would serve to show the world just how much God loves the world and how truly magnificent he is. There were a lot of rules to follow. Wanting to help them remember, God instructed his people to share this way of living with their children and to make this way of living a topic of conversation in daily life. As they walked on the road, and even as they fell asleep and woke up, the lifestyle God was calling them to was to be on their lips.

Then, for those who learn best through tactile experience, God said about the guidelines he'd given them for living,[6] "Tie them as symbols on your hands and bind them on your foreheads. Write them on the doorframes of your houses and on your gates" (Deut. 6:8–9). How much more up front and regular can you get?

They were far from perfect, but the Israelites approached both the practice of their religion and their relationship with God as a single and integral part of their lives. They saw no distinction between what you and I might categorize as either sacred or secular. They sought to live a daily life in which their work, rest, play, and worship were fully and completely integrated with one another—woven together with rituals, such as regular calls to prayer. There is no division between secular work and holy work for the children of God. Everything we do is sacred—because it all matters to God. The Israelites knew this and, as such, they approached the instruction of life in the faith as more than the passing on of information from one generation to the next. Their relationship with God was their identity. The same is true for us today. By centering the entirety of their lives around their identity as God's children, the Israelites were vigilant about making God a part of their everyday experiences. They diligently taught their children, and reminded one another, to see and serve God in every aspect of life. All of life, every part of it, is sacred, and the nation of Israel understood this. They received their instruction from God with reverence and they took it seriously. They still do today. I can close my eyes right now and picture the mezuzah nailed to the doorframe of a friend's home where I would visit as a child. And, even today, some Jewish people wear tefillin on their foreheads to remind them of God's desire for how they should live—his guidelines for living.

Hundreds of years after God handed down to his children these guidelines for living, Jesus would declare that the entire point of it all was for us, as God's people, to learn to love God with everything that is in us and to love our neighbors as we love ourselves. Then, just to be sure we were clear about who exactly our neighbor might be, Jesus told the story of the good Samaritan. Once again, the message is clear: We are called to love everyone. Period. No exceptions.

Together in the Year of Jubilee

At the very beginning of Jesus's ministry, on the Sabbath, Jesus pronounced the advent of the revolution. He made his way to the synagogue in Nazareth, as was his custom. There, in the synagogue, Jesus read some words from the scroll of the prophet Isaiah. Hundreds of years before, when Isaiah penned those words, the Israelites were exiles in Babylon. Isaiah's words spoke to the Israelites of a future day, when debts would be canceled, slaves would be set free, and property would be returned to its original owner. It would be a Year of Jubilee, and someone great would arrive on the scene to usher in this new era—an era of grace and reconciliation. These were the words Jesus read and, after reading these words from the prophet, Jesus handed the scroll back to the attendant. Then, with all eyes on him, Jesus sat down and said, "Today this scripture is fulfilled in your hearing" (Luke 4:21).

On this particular Sabbath day written about in the Gospel of Luke, hundreds of years after Isaiah predicted a season of grace, Jesus proclaimed those words were fulfilled. Jesus didn't say the words were *being* fulfilled. He said, "This scripture *is* fulfilled" (emphasis mine).

In Isaiah's original proclamation, the sentence immediately following the one about the year of the Lord's favor reads like this: "and the day of vengeance of our God" (Isa. 61:2). It is significant that Jesus folded up the scroll and sat down without including that portion of the proclamation in his teaching for the day. *Right now* is the moment of grace.

This is where we find ourselves: in the Year of Jubilee—the space between what has been and what will be. The Year of Jubilee finds us between an era of longing for our Savior and the day of God's judgment. We live where light encroaches on the darkness and everyone is welcome. *Right now* is the year of the Lord's favor, and the kingdom of God is slowly overtaking the kingdom of this world. Light is snuffing out the darkness, even though it may be difficult to detect this truth in the everydayness of our ordinary lives. Hope is winning over fear, mercy is overpowering violence, love is conquering hate.

When we base our analysis on what we see around us every day—polarization, fed by an abundance of terrifying trending topics and our own penchant for the dramatic—it's easy to believe we are living in the worst of times. Our focus turns to the waves of culture and crisis crashing all around us and we, quite naturally, shift into survival mode, forgetting we've been given life forever and doubting God is strong enough to pull us through the storm. We need someone to blame for our distress. We need an object to embody our fear. We are like Peter, once so confident and then suddenly overcome by fear and doubt. We cry out, "Lord, save me!" (Matt. 14:30).

It is hard to remember that the kind of love we are called to makes no exceptions and leaves no one out. The love of God saves *us*. Together. To make that message clear to us, again, God sent the Holy Spirit in that mysterious encounter on Pentecost. The disciples, we are told, were all together, in one place (see Acts 2:1).

This is who we are. We are together people. We are in-one-place people. We need to keep reminding ourselves of this. We are our tribe. All of us. Together. We need to keep reminding one another. I need you to remind me. You need me to remind you.

THREE

WHAT DO WE DO ABOUT EVIL AND INJUSTICE?

The heart bleeds, but vengeance belongs to the Creator.
—Arthur Redcloud, as Hikuc, in *The Revenant*

As we consider unity and oneness, we cannot avoid the reality of evil and injustice in our world. What do we do when the other party isn't interested in unity? What about those who won't or can't reconcile? As has already been made clear, we may think about this from an individualistic perspective, like when our spouse cheats on us or our employer demotes us or our friends turn their backs on us. But we also may think about it from a collective standpoint, such as the perspectives of indigenous people, African Americans, Japanese Americans, refugees, and so many others. In the United States, we remember those who have suffered great offenses in this country but have not been extended a full apology or an offer of reconciliation. In a global context, we remember survivors of the Holocaust and the Rwandan genocide, and we remember the stories of Syrian refugees, and so many others. When a mother's child is murdered and the killers go free, what then? What is the role of justice in these situations? And what is the responsibility of people of faith? Is forgiveness more important than justice? How does a person find the ability to forgive when the injustice continues?

The Sacrament of Giving Space

One day I asked these questions to a group of my friends, and one of them gently pointed me to a website where I could register for a weekend retreat called "The Gift of Reconciliation." I signed up, and a few weeks later I packed my suitcase and headed to the retreat, which was led by Father Mauritius Wilde.

Fr. Mauritius approached the topic in a way that honored the sacredness of reconciliation. The faith tradition of Fr. Mauritius, a Benedictine monk, considers reconciliation a sacrament. In fact, at the retreat center, the signs directing conferees to what I've known (in my limited, Protestant worldview) as confession were printed with the word *reconciliation*. At the very end of the retreat, I approached Fr. Mauritius and said, "I just want to make sure I'm clear on this. In the Catholic tradition, reconciliation is considered a sacrament?" In his kind way, Fr. Mauritius looked at me and said yes.

In everyday language, a sacrament is an outward sign of inward grace. Imagine that. Grace, as it turns out, is an exquisitely beautiful gift from God. God extends grace to us and, once we have bathed in its astounding luxury, we are uniquely positioned to extend grace to others. The grace of God makes our salvation possible. Of course, you and I aren't in the business of saving people. That is God's work. The grace we extend to others, however, is a small way of letting God be God in the life of another person.

We can think of grace as giving space for God to get a person to the place where he wants them to be. When we step back to make a clear path, it creates room for God to step in and lead the way. Making, or giving, space isn't the same as abandonment. Remember, we are hanging in with one another. Giving space is an acknowledgment that no one has "arrived." No one has all the answers. Giving space honors the truth that God is calling each of us to himself, and he is perfectly capable of getting us to our destination. When we offer grace for each person's journey, we're saying, in essence, "I trust God to get you to the place where he wants you to be." Imagine the idea of reconciliation, the *process* of reconciliation, as the outward sign of inward grace—of trusting God to get each of us exactly to where he wants us to be. And, while God is doing the work of getting us there, we each get to practice loving one another—without condition or judgment.

Two Chairs

When Fr. Mauritius taught us about reconciliation, he rested his left hand just above his hip and in the small of his waist. His elbow stuck out at an angle behind him. From time to time, he referred to some notes he had typed on a page, but mostly, he stood before us and offered us . . . well . . . grace. His humility spoke of his trust in God on our behalf and his understanding that he wasn't there to persuade but, rather, to take a few steps with us on the journey.

At one point during the weekend retreat, Fr. Mauritius set two chairs at the front of the room. Standing in front of those two chairs, he invited us to consider one chair to be the seat of justice and the other the seat of mercy. We were intrigued, and I leaned forward in my seat a bit. Both seats, Fr. Mauritius told us, belong to God, and he is a God of both justice and mercy. God has the credentials to sit on both of those seats and perfectly administer both justice and mercy. No matter the situation, only God knows the whole truth because he, through Jesus, *is* Truth. However, we often perceive him as sitting only on the seat of judgment, high above us and looking down his nose in our direction, seeking to catch us in an act of sinfulness. We "get" God's grace (as best we can), but we don't often "see" God as sitting on the seat of mercy.

And so we think the judgment seat is where we belong too. When we face a situation that makes us estranged from another person, Fr. Mauritius offered that we might consider the incident an opportunity to hear and embrace God's invitation to us to move from the seat of judgment to the seat of mercy when viewing the other person. And then Fr. Mauritius did just that. He looked out at the group of twenty or so of us gathered in that room with the light shining in the windows and the two chairs at the front and said, "Who would like to try it?"

It was a pretty safe bet that a group of people who would set aside a weekend to talk about reconciliation might just include a few individuals who were carrying around a bit of unresolved conflict. But the room was silent for a heartbeat or two, and I began to wonder if Fr. Mauritius's bold experiment might end right there. I, of course, had ducked my head, hoping he wouldn't call on me and make me do it, but that would have defeated the point. Reconciliation, after all, is an invitation from a God whose character is love and not an obligation required to earn God's love. Reconciliation is a gift God offers to help us live a life of faith that leads to unity with others. While this unity is indeed God's will for us, he will not force us into it. When Jesus prayed for us in the garden, he was expressing a deep desire for our oneness. He knew the power that our unity would express to a broken and divided world. Reconciliation is one way for us to turn toward oneness, but it is also our choice. This was the choice Fr. Mauritius was offering us.

In that conference center, when I dared to peek out from the corner of my eye, I saw Fr. Mauritius, standing there in the front of the room, with a look that told me he was not at all worried about whether anyone would give the mercy seat a try. He understood the gift of grace in moments such as these.

Just then, from the back of the room, an older woman softly said, "I'll give it a try." And Fr. Mauritius stepped forward to welcome her to the front of the room.

Isn't that how it is? Isn't this the way reconciliation works best? Instead of twisting arms in an attempt at forceful compliance (which often results in only half-hearted cooperation, anyway), God stands before us and gently offers us a choice. In our relationships with one another, we can choose the mercy seat, or we can opt for the judgment seat. This is important to understand. We do have a choice in the matter. We don't have to choose to be merciful when someone offends us or betrays us or misuses us. And, in the same way, we are given the opportunity and freedom to choose to practice and pursue mercy, reconciliation, and unity, justice is an option too. But justice is tricky, isn't it?

When we set out to exact justice, there is always the risk of miscalculation. Driven by our emotions, we may mete out more than what is required to even the score. How do we know just how much justice is the exact, right amount? Limited by our perspective, we may target the wrong person or assign the incorrect value to an offense. Only God has a perfect track record with regard to justice. He is the only one who knows every detail of every situation that causes us pain and grief—even people's unspoken thoughts and motivations.

Considering the Risk

With us, there is always this particular trouble. Rarely, if ever, do we really want justice that only measures out evenly. We are not wired that way. When someone does us wrong, we want them to experience the pain and hurt we experienced, *plus a little bit more.*

Cain and Abel are our first examples of this expectation of escalating "payback." The story of these two brothers is told in eight verses in Genesis 4.

Cain was born first, to his parents, Adam and Eve. Later, Abel was born, and when he grew up he became a shepherd. His big brother, Cain, became a farmer and cultivated the earth. One day Cain and Abel each brought an offering to God. Cain brought an offering of "some" of his crops, while Abel brought the very best selections of firstborn lambs from his flock.

God was quite pleased with Abel's offering but less impressed by the offering presented by Cain. In fact, the Bible tells us God didn't even accept Cain's gift (v. 5). This "offering event" becomes the catalyst for disaster in the lives of Cain and Abel. It is the very first biblical account of our natural bent toward seeking revenge, which often exceeds the notion of taking an eye for an eye. Cain's dejection turned to anger, and God warned Cain of danger ahead, telling him that if he wasn't careful, his anger would get the best of him.

In fact, God looked at Cain, who had placed himself in the seat of judgment, and said, "Sin is crouching at the door; it desires to have you, but you must rule over it" (v. 7). God was offering an out for Cain. In essence, God was saying, "Hey, buddy. Move over. Let me sit there. You can sit right next to me, in this mercy seat. But let me sit in that seat today." But Cain ignored God's offer. Instead, he lured his brother into a field and killed him. Even with God's admonition to Cain to get his anger in check before it took control of him, Cain followed the path of retribution and revenge. We'll talk more about anger in another chapter, but for now, notice this sequence of emotions: Cain's embarrassment morphed into anger, and when his anger was left unchecked, it resulted in murder. Cain's actions toward his brother were beyond the scope of the injustice he suffered. Some say justice is punishment that fits the crime, but from our limited perspectives, it's difficult to know exactly how to measure that—either the full scope of the crime or the punishment it requires.

While we may miscalculate with regard to justice, we are in much safer territory when it comes to our risk with regard to mercy. When it comes to extending mercy, the risk is that we won't be received. The risk is that we lay our hearts bare and find ourselves rejected. But in the face of divisiveness and polarization, rejection is already on the table. That card has already been played. We have already been scorned or wounded or broken.

When we begin from the seat of mercy, however, we move ourselves out of the way, and we *make way* for God's perfect administration of justice. Moving to the mercy seat does not indicate a willingness to ignore justice altogether. No. Moving to the mercy seat acknowledges the truth that only God can administer justice perfectly. Moving to the mercy seat lets God be God.

A Long Journey to Grace

One of the most compelling stories of the healing and justice-inducing power of choosing mercy is the story of Immaculée Ilibagiza.

In 1994, Rwanda experienced an upheaval from which it is still reeling. Beginning on April 7, and lasting for approximately one hundred days, the Hutu population rose up and slaughtered many members of the Tutsi population. Up to one million Rwandans were killed. In many cases the murderers and victims had been friends, neighbors, and even family. Their children had attended school together, learning in the same classrooms and playing on the same playgrounds.

Tensions had been building between the two groups for decades. Some of the years leading up to this horrific genocide had been plagued with conflicts and seasons of violence. But those previous conflicts were small compared to the atrocities committed over the course of those one hundred days in 1994. Incited by the government and spurred on by what can only be described as the evil of extreme crowd mentality, ordinary Hutu citizens armed themselves with machetes, swords, and makeshift clubs. They hunted down their Tutsi neighbors and friends, and beat and hacked them to death, torturing them in the streets, burning down their homes, and mercilessly murdering their children—those born and unborn.

Immaculée Ilibagiza, along with seven other women, survived the massacre by hiding in a small bathroom in the home of a Hutu minister. They lived there for ninety-one long days and nights of terror, fear, and grave uncertainty. Ilibagiza tells her story in the book *Left to Tell: Discovering God Amidst the Rwandan Holocaust.* Of her six family members, only Immaculée and her brother—a student in Senegal at the time of the genocide—survived.

Not long after Immaculée was rescued and the genocide had ended, she went to the prison to meet with the man who led the gang that killed her mother and brother. While a Tutsi guard watched, the Hutu prisoner could barely raise his eyes to meet those of his victims' daughter and sister. The Hutu prisoner's name was Felicien, and this is what Immaculée writes of their encounter:

> Felicien was sobbing. I could feel his shame. He looked up at me for only a moment, but our eyes met. I reached out, touched his hands lightly, and quietly said what I'd come to say. "I forgive you."[1]

After suffering so much grief and loss, it's hard to believe this encounter. This was no cheap or quick forgiveness. A reading of Immaculée's story tells of her long journey—over the course of the harrowing days she spent in hiding—to the grace of mercy and forgiveness. Immaculée shares this account of one small part of her journey, which took place one day while she was hiding in the bathroom from those who wished to kill her:

> One night I heard screaming not far from the house, and then a baby crying. The killers must have slain the mother

and left her infant to die in the road. The child wailed all night; by morning, its cries were feeble and sporadic, and by nightfall, it was silent. I heard dogs snarling nearby and shivered as I thought about how that baby's life had ended. I prayed for God to receive the child's innocent soul, and then asked Him, How can I forgive people who would do such a thing to an infant?

I heard His answer as clearly as if we'd been sitting in the same room chatting: You are all My children . . . and the baby is with Me now.

It was such a simple sentence, but it was the answer to the prayers I'd been lost in for days . . . In God's eyes, the killers were part of His family, deserving of love and forgiveness. I knew that I couldn't ask God to love me if I were unwilling to love His children. At that moment, I prayed for the killers, for their sins to be forgiven . . .

I took a crucial step toward forgiving the killers that day. My anger was draining from me—I'd opened my heart to God, and He'd touched it with His infinite love. For the first time, I pitied the killers. I asked God to forgive their sins and turn their souls toward His beautiful light.

That night I prayed with a clear conscience and a clean heart. For the first time since I entered the bathroom, I slept in peace.[2]

This way that Jesus teaches us to live feels backward and illogical. But he was serious. He didn't say, "If you want to give this a try, maybe it will help to love your enemies and pray for the people who make your life difficult." There is no way around the direction Jesus calls us to take. Love, and its expression of mercy, is the way of the cross. This is the pathway to hope, healing, and redemption. As Immaculée writes, "The love of a single heart can make a world of difference."[3]

Remember that God is the God of both justice *and* mercy. Sometimes God works out his justice through the judicial system or through other public venues. Other times he works out his justice in quiet conversations with those who have wronged us. Sometimes we play an active role in his work of justice, and sometimes we may not even perceive our role. And sometimes God doesn't involve us at all.

Defining Justice

What is justice? When, for example, a mother's child is murdered, some would say justice would be for the murderer to meet the same fate. Or, at the very least, face a future that includes no prospect of freedom and none of the regular comforts usually associated with a life of freedom. How could anyone possibly propose something different, in light of such a cruel crime? How could anyone ask that mother to create space in her heart where forgiveness overrides injustice and reconciliation grants freedom? It's preposterous!

And so, we don't. It is not our place to make such a demand. We don't work out our own reconciliation through the grief and anguish of someone else's situation. We are called instead to grieve with those who grieve and rejoice with those who rejoice. Indeed, the day may come when reconciliation is desired or justice is sought. But in the moment of grief, we grieve too.

Reconciliation begins in our own hearts and minds. Inside our individual souls. Often it is facilitated by outside forces: counselors, spiritual advisors, family members, friends, support groups, recovery groups, and other sources of help and healing. Ultimately, however, reconciliation and oneness—the oneness Christ desires for us—is the result of deeply spiritual work, accomplished in times of solitary reflection, synthesized by the power of the Holy Spirit, and often borne out in the midst of chaotic upheaval. But it is always deeply personal work. It is the work of faith. I once heard an Episcopal priest express it this way: "A life of faith is a life of risk, to hasten the kingdom and fix fracture in the world."

Ours is a field guide of *kingdom come*, where justice is not a prerequisite for reconciliation and oneness. Instead, justice flows forth from the two, as the natural consequence and gloriously defiant result of the fulfillment of Christ's prayer in the garden. The unified body of Christ—her individual members reconciled to themselves, to God, and to one another—is the exactly unique and perfectly equipped environment for the incubation of justice so many of us crave. But let's be clear about this justice we seek.

In his book *No Future without Forgiveness*, Bishop Desmond Tutu writes about the work of the Truth and Reconciliation Commission of South Africa. As he establishes the foundation of the book and sets out to walk the reader through the work of the commission, Bishop Tutu is careful to make the distinction between retributive justice and restorative justice. Retributive justice, he says, is justice "whose chief goal is to be punitive, so that the wronged party is really the state, something impersonal, which has little consideration for the real victims and almost none for the perpetrator." He goes on to say,

> We contend that there is another kind of justice, restorative justice . . . Here the central concern is not retribution or punishment . . . the central concern is the healing of breaches, the redressing of imbalances, the restoration of broken relationships, a seeking to rehabilitate both the victim and perpetrator,

who should be given the opportunity to be reintegrated into the community he has injured by his offense. This is a far more personal approach, regarding the offense as something that has happened to persons and whose consequence is a rupture in relationships. Thus we would claim that justice, restorative justice, is being served when efforts are being made to work for healing, for forgiving, and for reconciliation.[4]

Let's not get suckered by the glitz of retributive justice, when we are people of the God of restoration. Let's not settle for an eye-for-eye form of justice when Christ has clearly taught us something more. Here's how he put it:

> You have heard that it was said, "Eye for eye, and tooth for tooth." But I tell you, do not resist an evil person. If anyone slaps you on the right cheek, turn to them the other cheek also. And if anyone wants to sue you and take your shirt, hand over your coat as well. If anyone forces you to go one mile, go with them two miles. Give to the one who asks you, and do not turn away from the one who wants to borrow from you.
> You have heard that it was said, "Love your neighbor and hate your enemy." But I tell you, love your enemies and pray for those who persecute you, that you may be children of your Father in heaven. He causes his sun to rise on the evil and the good, and sends rain on the righteous and the unrighteous. If you love those who love you, what reward will you get? Are not even the tax collectors doing that? And if you greet only your own people, what are you doing more than others? Do not even pagans do that? Be perfect, therefore, as your heavenly Father is perfect. (Matt. 5:38–48)

In the purview of this passage, retributive justice sounds like an easy out. But we are not called to the easy way out, are we? Perhaps, in the scheme of things, retributive justice has its place. But there is a sense in which retributive justice falls short of the vision God has for us and the reason Christ died for us.

Christ died for us *while we were yet sinners*, not after we got our act together. He prepares a table before us *in the presence of our enemies*. He is not only our rescue, he is also our refuge. Long before the dust settled—in the absence of reparations and in the wake of our long disobedience and casting off of our affections toward him—God sent his Son so that we might be *justified*. When retributive justice was our reasonable inheritance, we were given grace instead. What we deserve is a justice that is punitive and impersonal, but what we receive in its place is mercy.

Restorative justice, even in the face of the very worst evil, is justice that looks like this: the kingdom of God, encroaching on the kingdom of this world—a kingdom of darkness whose ruler has been doomed from the start. The practice of this kind of justice is no offhand, second-rate, spur-of-the-moment endeavor. This kind of justice is sacrificial.

Mercy Seat

The woman at our retreat who chose to try out the mercy seat was sitting in the very last row. She had one of those fancy walkers—the kind with wheels, brakes, and a basket. That walker required a wide berth, so those of us in the classroom did what we could to clear a path for her. We stood back and moved the chairs and tables so that this woman could make her way to the front of the room to sit in the mercy seat.

The Sister (as it turns out she was, indeed, a Catholic nun) lowered herself to the mercy seat, and then Fr. Mauritius took one step back and turned to face her. "So," he said to her gently, "what might you be thinking, there on the mercy seat?"

In a quiet voice, she said she had been holding on to a grudge for decades. She didn't tell us the details. That wasn't necessary. She simply intimated at a falling out she'd had with another Sister, many, many years before. She told us she hadn't been able to let it go. But now, in just the few minutes she'd spent looking at a decades-long conflict from the vantage point of mercy, she said, "This whole thing has probably affected her as well." And just like that, we could see that God had led that Sister to exactly where he wanted her to be.

God does not ignore our broken hearts when he invites us to consider mercy. He isn't even telling us to choose mercy *instead of* justice. But where we are often geared toward revenge and payback in regard to our version of justice, God is always working toward restoration. God's goal is always unity and healing, oneness and reconciliation, so he invites us to begin with mercy.

God invites us to begin with mercy because that's what he has done for us. He isn't telling us to move on or buck up or just get over it already. In the mercy seat rests the power of God to heal our deepest hurts. When we engage others from a position of brokenness and hurt, we risk causing more brokenness and hurt. Moving from the seat of justice and into the seat of mercy has the power to short-circuit hatred, hostility, and hopelessness. Choosing to view a person or a situation through the lens of compassion (which is another way of talking about mercy) makes space for the possibility of oneness and unity.

Of course, it would be wrong to have a discussion of justice without including the words of the prophet Micah. His oft-quoted words remind us that God requires justice of us.

"What does the LORD require of you?" This is the question God asks his children through the words of the prophet. The answer is one we often repeat—on T-shirts, in worship songs, and inked in tattoos. "To act justly," the Lord entreats us, and to "love mercy and walk humbly with your God" (Mic. 6:8). These words fell like rain on the shoulders of a nation called to represent God to the world, in the world. But in the book of Micah, we find that God's people were guilty of grave and repeated injustices. In the book of Micah, we find that God has an offense against the people. This is not about human beings offending one another. Instead, this is an exchange between our holy God and his children—children who had turned their backs on God and had begun worshiping idols. The concept of God having an offense against God's people is a concept that recognizes that God's people had missed the mark. They had been found guilty—injustice and ingratitude were their crimes. As is the custom of each and every one of us, God's people had lost their way.

Convicted of their wrong, they desired a way back to him. They wanted reconciliation and feared the prospect of any alternative. "How do we fix this?" Faced with the gravity of their wrongdoing, they wanted to know how to get right with God again. They dreamed up extravagant options: burnt offerings, year-old calves, thousands of rams, rivers of oil. In desperation, they blindly offered up their firstborn children. Like Felicien, the Hutu prisoner who faced Immaculée in shame, the children of God could not lift their faces in God's direction.

Then, speaking through the prophet, God reminded them of where they had lost their way. God reminded them—the same way so many parents remind their children as they grab the car keys and head out the door—"Don't forget, you represent our family to the world." God reminded them that, as his representatives in the world, he needs us to *do* justice. In our dealings with people each day—wherever we find ourselves—we must deal with them fairly. Matthew Henry describes this justice by saying, "We must do justly, must render to all their due, according as our relation and obligation to them are; *we must do wrong to none, but do right to all, in their bodies, goods, and good name"* (emphasis mine).[5] This, in a sense, is preemptive justice. It is the way we are called to move through the world, doing our best to limit the possibility of offense. "If it is possible, as far as it depends on you," Paul writes, "live at peace with everyone" (Rom. 12:18). This is mercy. It is the posture of compassion.

Compassion is the precursor to restorative justice. Compassion invites us to engage our estrangement through the lens of a shared humanity. In *Just Mercy*, Bryan Stevenson reminds us "there is no wholeness outside of our reciprocal humanity."[6] We are, it turns out, all in this together. It might not seem as if we'll get there together, but we've got the prayer of Jesus to guide us. So, as a beloved pastor used to say, it's worth pressing on "to see what the end will be."

In the end, as we saw in the case of the nun at that retreat, mercy and compassion change *us*. Even early scientific studies seem to bear this out, revealing that the practice of compassion results in the shrinking of the amygdala in the brain.[7] The amygdala houses our fight-or-flight response. Early studies show that exercising the compassion "muscles" in our brains pushes out the innate and ancient responses in us that cause us to run away from people who appear to pose a threat to us. This is important because a lot of our division is the result of misinterpreting a difference of opinion or perspective as a "threat." In a world that runs quite hard on fear, we forget God's constant reminder to us to *fear not*. It is true that very real and present dangers exist in this world. The work of those who would seek wisdom and discernment is not to love our lives so much that we cannot love our neighbor. We make things right when we *see* things right. We move with compassion when we view things and people through the lenses of grace and love.

Sometimes we don't care about that though. Sometimes we want our enemy to suffer for the pain they've caused us. This is normal. This is human. The emotions that accompany adversity and unspeakable grief are fierce in their power over us. God did not tell us not to get angry. Anger is an emotion, just like all the rest. It is normal, and it is healthy. Trying to "not get angry" is like trying not to be proud at your child's graduation. What we've been instructed to do is to refrain from sinning in the midst of our anger and as a result of it. Where anger often makes us feel as if some sort of outward action is required, the truth is much closer to the heart. Anger often calls us inward, but it calls so loudly and fiercely that our instinct makes us lash out—sometimes at others and sometimes at ourselves. The journey to mercy is so often two steps forward and one step back. Some situations are easier for us, while others require more patience, more endurance, more surrender, and more sacrifice. So don't beat yourself up if you can't see your way to mercy and compassion. You are not alone. In fact, you are in very good company, and revolution is on the way.

FOUR

LET IT GO

I had been short with the lady at the car rental counter. Not mean, exactly. But not really nice either. Her name was Aneata. Just like that. "Neat" with an "a" on each end. I did not really want to be there. I was on my way to speak to a group of women and was looking forward to getting a break from talking about unity and oneness. I was tired of unity and oneness—and all the talking about them. I'd had enough of all the conversations about police brutality and unarmed black men and who gets to say what about which lives matter. I was tired of extending grace and answering emails and private messages asking for my take on a sound bite or an article or a few words someone had written on social media. I was exhausted by all of it, to be honest. I was without hope. I didn't want to be one with people anymore.

Standing at the car rental counter, I was grumpy. I'd had to wake up at 4 a.m. to make my early flight. I am not a morning person, so all I really wanted was to get to my car. I wanted a car that was quiet and clean. One that smelled brand new. One that would sync with my phone so I could let the navigation system kindly instruct me regarding miles and turns and direction, while I zoned out behind the wheel.

But Aneata was too nice for that. She stood on the other side of the counter and smiled at me from over the top of her red-framed spectacles, which rested calmly—Aneata style—on the end of her nose. I was doomed from the start.

"Where are you headed today?" Aneata asked me as she made herself look preoccupied with whatever was happening on her computer screen.

"Oh, I have a two and a half hour drive ahead of me," I answered, not feeling up to a small-talk session.

"OK," she said. *She is good at this,* I thought, against my will. *She probably prays each morning before she heads out to work. She probably prays for the customers she'll encounter throughout the day.* I spied a small, unspectacular cross hanging from an unpretentious chain around her neck. But, honestly, that cross could mean anything, right?

"So are you going to visit family?" Aneata smiled at me.

"No. No," I answered. "I'm going to . . ." and this is where things always have the potential to fall apart. Like when people ask me how I came to live in Nebraska, of all places, and I say, "My husband's job." Then they ask, "Oh, what does he do?" And I know my next words have to be: "He's a pastor." I say each word carefully. But not in a way that sounds as if I'm being careful, because that would make it worse. I try to make it sound the same as whatever it is they might do for a living (which it is, for all work is holy) because, once it's out there, things change—sometimes for the good, but mostly the conversations become awkward. And then I try, awkwardly, to ease the awkwardness, which only makes things more awkward.

"I'm going to speak at an event," I said.

"Nice," she said.

Whew! I thought. And then . . .

"What kind of event?" Aneata asked, handing me my license and credit card over the counter. I slid my card into my wallet and surrendered to this early morning work of being drawn out of myself at the airport car rental counter. My shoulders dropped, and I let my defensiveness slide off onto the linoleum tiles. I returned Aneata's warm smile with my weak one. I'd been caught—defenses up, tension high, nerves frayed. "I've been invited to speak at a women's retreat," I said.

"Mmmmm . . ." Aneata replied, her eyes on her computer monitor. Aneata wasn't alone behind the counter. Her coworkers were there too. Each one of them, from what I had picked up from snippets of their conversations, was just as warm and gracious as Aneata. I'd been watching as they greeted one another with a level of affection that felt more familial than functional. They engaged their customers the same way Aneata was engaging me: gentle, respectful, and reaching for something that might lie just beneath the surface, but in a way that felt welcome and not a violation. Getting us in a rental car and on our way to our destination felt more like a means to an end than the end itself. Connecting people with a vehicle seemed to be the vehicle they were using to, I don't know, bless us, or something. *Maybe they all prayed before they came to work each day. Maybe they even prayed together*, I thought. Who knows?

I guess in some part of my consciousness I hold out hope that people are praying for me. But even with this hope in my heart, it's clear I must not really anticipate I will actually be on the receiving end of that kind of grace—the grace someone prayed they might be able to demonstrate toward me, before they even knew me.

"So what are you going to speak about?" Aneata asked me. We were covering many difficult questions in our very first encounter with each other. I think these are the most difficult questions to answer, no matter the situation. "What's your talk about?" "What are you *going* to talk about?" "What *did* you talk about?" These are akin to their equally disorienting yet deeply sincere and well-meaning cousin, "What's your book about?" The answers to these questions seem simple enough. The questions are not meant to be difficult. They are meant to show interest and maybe even reveal some point of connection. But these *are* hard questions to answer.

"I'm going to talk about God," I told Aneata.

It was a make-it-or-break-it answer. Like telling people my husband is a minister. It's vague but also specific. It opens a door but could close a few. It speaks volumes but also might generate more questions. "I'm going to tell the women how much God loves them," I said, unprompted by Aneata.

"We need that," she said, keeping the Truth generalized, the way a counselor or a priest or a minister might. Her co-worker looked at us from the corner of his eye. Just then, another man behind the counter, talking with his co-workers, let out the most beautiful sound. It was sparkling and bright and soulful and free and sincere and true and unashamed. He was laughing. Was he laughing at something someone said? It was hard to be sure from my side of the counter. But he seemed to have burst open with joy—and this man had been gifted with a glorious laugh.

"*That*," I said, "is the best laugh ever!"

The kindness and joy of these workers at a car rental counter in a bustling, metropolitan airport was washing away my gruff exterior. I felt my travel-weary self begin to come to life again. It was a tiny resurrection. Someone had hit the reset button on my soul. In fact, another of Aneata's co-workers said that very thing. He had been watching and listening to Aneata and me. He looked at me and said, "Like a reset button, right?"

"That's right," I said. "A reset button." I was talking metaphorically, but the true meaning of my words was more like, "Bless me, Father, for I have sinned."

I'd brought my grumpy self with my ugly attitude into these people's space, and they had returned my gruffness with grace. They provided the opportunity for God to reach through and warm my heart—and the laughter had been the clincher. The car rental people were my confessors, and they humbly wore their cassocks—which looked like red polyester vests—as they willingly listened to me. And maybe they *had* prayed together that morning. But maybe not.

"Maybe I can do for these women what you've all done for me here, today," I said.

"All right, now," Aneata's co-worker said, waving his hand in my direction. Aneata slid my paperwork over to me and said, "It's all good," which sounded a lot to me like, "Your sins are forgiven. Go in peace."

We all need confessors. We need people who will take us as we are and let us be that way. We need people who won't try to change us simply because we've shown them that we know we can be improved on. We need people who receive our sincere apology and let it be just that. "My bad," we say. And they say, "It's all good." And mean it.

The Sacred Work of an Honest and True Apology

Confession doesn't always lead to reconciliation. Even in cases where confessions are accompanied by apologies, it doesn't always lead to oneness. But that doesn't mean we should stop engaging these sacred practices. Often the person offering an honest and true apology or making a confession has worked extremely hard to get to the point of owning up to their failures, shortcomings, and missteps. Humbly admitting their guilt is often the end of a long journey for that person.

On June 26, 2015, George Robertson, senior pastor at First Presbyterian Church in Augusta, Georgia, wrote an essay titled "We . . . and Our Fathers Have Sinned." Based on Daniel 9:8, the essay was posted on the church's website. Here's an excerpt:

> As white members and leaders of evangelical churches, we must repent of our passivity and/or proactivity during the dark days of our Nation's Jim Crow era. We must repent of our passivity: our sins of omission in which we failed to seek justice, follow the golden rule, and resist the cultural temptation to hoard power. But we must also repent of our activity: the ways that we actively contributed to and participated in the sinful and exclusionary culture of the day both knowingly and unknowingly. Jesus said that whether or not you are actually guilty of offending your brother, if/when you learn that he has something against you, you must "get going" and pursue reconciliation with him. Even if you are in the middle of a worship service, you must "leave your gift and be reconciled to your brother." Through the decades, we have learned that our African-American brothers rightly have "something against us." In their years of struggle, even to the present day, we have failed to validate their oppression and at times have contributed to it.[1]

I've been engaged in conversations about race in the Church in America for many years. These conversations often go around in circles with people taking sides and building up walls. George Robertson's essay feels something like forward movement, and I worry that people may invalidate Robertson's perspective or poke holes in his argument.

Sincerely apologizing for something is hard work, and accepting an apology is a holy and sacred charge.

When Jesus taught us how to pray, he included these words: "Forgive us . . . as we also have forgiven" (Matt. 6:12). When we go to God seeking forgiveness, he is quick to forgive. He doesn't keep a record of our faults and failings. He extends forgiveness to us and continues to woo each of us back to himself.

We do not forgive as quickly as God; we are human, after all. But perhaps we can remember how hard it is for someone to confess and/or apologize, and let that stand for something.

George Robertson made an apology. He confessed his complicity in systems that have oppressed, silenced, or marginalized African Americans. There is no way he will ever be able to apologize to every single person who has felt the sting of racism in America. However, I find his apology to be profoundly moving on many levels: He named the offense. He took ownership of the offense. He validated the lament of those who were offended. He is working to make it right, as much as it depends on him.

Christians get it wrong sometimes. Often our claims of having a deep love for Jesus are the exact reasons we can't see our sins clearly. Our vision gets clouded by a desire for power or comfort or safety or riches or reputation. Then we hide our flawed perspective behind the cross of Jesus. It happens all the time. History has revealed the many ways humanity has justified its wrongs by draping sin in Scripture and hiding complicity in the cross rather than nailing it there. By justifying our sin in the very person who came to free us from it, we entrench ourselves in a false understanding of both our Savior and our commissioning. When we use Jesus and Scripture to justify our sinful convictions, we have made Jesus in our own image and we have made our convictions our idol. We cannot let Satan, our only true enemy, manipulate us into corrupting the message of the gospel so that it fits our agenda and misrepresents the power of Jesus to unite us across a plethora of differences. If our holy convictions require us to make enemies of others, malign others, dehumanize others, or otherwise minimize another person's humanity, it's time to check in and see if we're truly serving the Jesus of the Bible.

A faith that uses Jesus to justify any type of division, prejudice, injustice, or superiority needs to be examined and brought back into alignment with the truth of Christ's message of good news. The litmus test is to regularly offer up our heart, soul, mind, and strength to the scrutiny of the Holy Spirit. King David, in the Psalms, laid it out for us when he asked God to search his thoughts and his heart for anything that might be offensive to God (Ps. 139). Ultimately, this is where the buck stops. The way we live out our faith should bring honor and pleasure to God—never offense. We have the benefit of hindsight to show us that we had it wrong in so many of our historic moments and decisions. We can see how our collective vision was clouded and how our convictions took the place of Christ as the object of our worship. Hindsight helps us recognize where we failed to love (particularly those we christened our enemies). We tell ourselves to recite our history to the generations that follow us so they won't repeat our mistakes. But we must constantly hold our own convictions loosely before the transformative power of the Spirit of God. Over and over again, we have to allow ourselves to be transformed by letting God renew our minds. If it's been awhile since your faith was challenged, I'd humbly submit that you may have drawn too tight a circle around your convictions and cordoned at least part of yourself off from the sweetly fragrant power of the Holy Spirit.

God Is Not a Prisoner of Culture

Our God is not a prisoner of culture. An intriguing story is told in Acts 10, which Peter witnessed firsthand. In this biblical account, God told him that Peter was free from the dietary restrictions that had been given to the Jews. Peter had found a quiet place to pray, on the roof or balcony of a house in Joppa. It was around lunchtime and, as you may have experienced in your own prayer time, Peter's mind wandered to what he might have for lunch. He became so distracted that he fell into a trance. In this frame of mind, Peter saw the skies open and a sheet seemed to float from heaven and rest on the ground. On the blanket was every kind of animal a person could imagine, and Peter heard the voice of God saying to eat whatever he wanted.

Now, Peter came from a long tradition of learning the laws handed down to the Jews from God during the Exodus. Surely these dietary restrictions—and the consequences of breaking them—had been drilled into Peter's head. It's not easy to break free from that kind of indoctrination. Peter's response was perfectly reasonable. He said, "No way! I've never eaten food that isn't kosher!" But God insisted. He told Peter three times that it was perfectly fine to eat the food before him on the blanket. Peter was dumbfounded. I imagine he felt a lot like many people who were raised in households in which they were taught—whether outright or through attitudes they picked up on—that sex is bad. These children learn that sex is not to be spoken of, thought of, or enjoyed. Until, suddenly, on their wedding night, they are expected to engage in sex without inhibition and with inexplicable pleasure. Of course, sex is not bad. And neither is food. Both are delectable gifts from God. And, while this metaphor may be a bit extreme, it should help to point out how difficult it sometimes is to let go of a long-held conviction once the Holy Spirit reveals his true intent for us. In both of these examples—food and sex—the focus is on something more than the object or physical act.

In the Old Testament, God used food restrictions as one way to help establish the Jews' trust in him and in one another. After Jesus's death, the veil of the temple was torn in two, symbolizing that a relationship with God was possible for everyone, not just the Jews. The good news had been entrusted to the biological descendants of Abraham, and God had established his Church on Peter's confession that Jesus is the Christ (see Matt. 16:16). Now God was commissioning the Church to get the word out to the ends of the earth. If the gospel was to be shared across cultures and countries and continents, God could not let food restrictions stand in the way. Even though the food God had forbidden the Jews to eat was not inherently bad, it was hard for Peter and others to make that distinction. I can imagine quite a few well-intentioned Israelite parents, desperately trying to keep their rambunctious and inquisitive children from eating restricted foods. It's hard to explain to a five-year-old that God has asked certain things of them, so the parents may have simply said, while pulling the child away from the bacon stand in the open-air market, "No, Peter! That food is bad! We don't eat that!" It's the same way modern parents tell children sex is bad. The intent is good, but it often results in associations that are hard to deconstruct.

Three times on the rooftop, God said to Peter, "No, seriously. I'm telling you. This food is not bad. I know what I said before about not eating it. But that was because I wanted you to learn to obey and trust me. It wasn't about the food. Now, though, I'm going to be asking you to share the good news with people who aren't even Jewish, and that means you're going to have to get comfortable eating food like this. You're going to be in their homes and become friends with them. So that means lots of meals together!" Three times, Peter told God, "No way, man! That food is bad! We don't eat that stuff!" After the third time (three times was pretty much a theme with Peter and the Lord), the blanket and all of the food were lifted into the heavens again and Peter was left wondering what in the world had just happened. Was this for real? How was he going to just start eating bacon and shellfish after all these years? It was a paradigm shift for sure.

God had not changed. Instead, God was asking Peter to trust him even more than ever before. God was teaching Peter something about himself and his kingdom that he had never before shared with Peter. This is the way of things. Sometimes we get entrenched in some conviction about God and what we believe he thinks about something based on what we have come to understand about him in that moment in time. Sometimes we get entrenched in some conviction about God and what we believe he thinks about something based on what he has revealed to us about himself. But God is far too complex to contain in our conventional wisdom or our modern sensibilities. Instead of conforming to culture, God is continually influencing culture. God is like an exquisite diamond, with multiple facets we can never take in at one time. He reveals a facet of himself to us, and if we are lucky, he might one day reveal another facet of himself to us. And all the while, God is revealing different facets of himself to each of us. Each of us has only a stunningly gorgeous yet short and complex glimpse of our great God. That's it.

It might be the case that God is trying to show you some facet of himself you've never seen before. I've had that happen to me. I've got a few examples in mind, but I'll share just one. For years I rooted myself in a certain conviction about a certain thing. It doesn't matter what that conviction was. But I was sure I was fighting the Lord's battle regarding that particular conviction. I was convinced I was in the Lord's army, and we were marching to Zion. Beautiful, beautiful Zion. I pitted myself against people who were in a different "camp." I spoke disparagingly about them to anyone who would listen. I was nice to their faces and evil behind their backs. If anyone called me on my behavior, I pointed them to what the *Word of God* (I envisioned it in italics) had to say about it. That shut them down, but not because of my great elucidation of the Scriptures. I was so ridiculously abrasive about the whole thing. No matter how many Bible verses I spewed out, what spoke louder than anything was my lack of love for the people I'd deemed unworthy. What spoke loudly was my distorted and finite view of God, who is all and only and ever love.

When God begins to reveal a new way of looking at the world, he's actually showing me the world through his eyes. He's giving me the mind of Christ I have prayed for. He's transforming me by renewing my mind. The trouble, of course, is that I pray for God to make me more like Jesus, but I don't really know what that means. I am confounded when I find out Jesus looks more like my least favorite person in the world than I ever thought possible. I am confused when I discover God's ways really are not the same as my ways and God's thoughts are not like my thoughts. God, it turns out, is holy, and I have no idea what that means. I thought I did. I thought my convictions were holy, but instead they were divisive, loud, proud, and scared. They were puny. They were not holy. Even though I thought they were. I thought God was pleased with me and my convictions. And, because God loves me, God brought someone into my everyday life who loved Jesus but hailed from that other "camp." God does not let us maintain our jacked-up way of seeing the world and use that perspective as propaganda for him. Nope.

The nature of my relationship with this person from the other camp made it necessary for us to interact on a regular basis. We spent a lot of hours together and had a lot of conversations. Thank God (and I mean that) I never spoke my convictions aloud to this person. Although, who am I kidding? My convictions were probably written all over my face. My convictions took form through my body language. And yet, over time, as I'm sure God ordained it, I began to see the value in this person. I began to see the love this person had for Jesus and for other people. All people. I began to see I had fallen way short of loving this person the way God asked me to. As God worked through this person to transform me, I became less and less concerned about fighting that particular battle. I began to understand that love does not necessarily require a battle from me. Love loves. Period.

In Peter's case, God brought a man named Cornelius—someone from another camp, a different race—to confirm the message he'd been trying to get Peter to accept on the rooftop with the sheet of food. Cornelius was a devout man. He held a prominent position as captain of the Italian Guard. He loved God and was generous and kind to those in his community. The day before Peter went back and forth with God about the sheet filled with food, Cornelius had a vision of his own. In his vision, Cornelius was told to send some men to Joppa to find Peter and invite the apostle to his house. The next day, Cornelius did as he had been instructed. So while Peter sat there on the roof, stunned and hungry, three men showed up at the door and invited Peter to Cornelius's house.

Anyone who has spent any time reading anything about Peter knows he didn't have much of a filter. He just sort of said whatever came to his mind. Once Peter got to Cornelius's place and had been welcomed and settled in, he said, "You know, I'm sure that this is highly irregular. Jews just don't do this—visit and relax with people of another race" (Acts 10:28 Message). And then, the confession: "But God has just shown me that no race is better than any other" (v. 29). In other words, Peter was saying, "I've been wrong about the way I have viewed people who are not Jewish. God has shown me how he sees things, and I'm being transformed because of it." Peter realized God doesn't play favorites, and Cornelius served as Peter's confessor. The good news is for everyone. And not only that: it was okay to eat the food! Once Peter realized this, he told Cornelius all he had learned and seen while Jesus was with them. And, as Peter got done speaking, the Holy Spirit filled the place and everyone there who was listening.

No one has all the information available about God and what he thinks about the things of this world. If we let our convictions take the place of Jesus in our lives, we could very well be standing in the way of the same Holy Spirit with whom we profess to be filled. If God is calling you to loosen your grip on a few of your convictions, let them go. Please. Let them go. God can handle the fallout. And whatever fallout comes from letting God transform you by the renewing of your mind is nothing compared to the fallout from standing in the way of the Holy Spirit. Let it go.

FIVE

THE POWER TO UNITE

Before and above everything else, we are loved by God. All of us. Even those who don't claim to be, as well as those who don't believe they are. We are all loved by God, created in his image. God's love extends even to our enemies. God's love for us is wildly unconditional and staggeringly deep. That, above all else, is first and foremost the most important thing to understand.

The next thing is that those who follow Jesus and are People of the Way (you may call it being "born again" or "saved" or "Christian") are Christ's ambassadors. In other words, we are not citizens of this world. In a very real sense, we are aliens here. Wherever we go, we represent the kingdom of God, which is where our true citizenship rests. Many would argue that the kingdom of God is a place we're all trying to get to. But when Jesus taught the disciples to pray, he was teaching us all to pray as if the kingdom might be made manifest right here on earth. *"Your kingdom come, your will be done, on earth as it is in heaven."*[1]

What a powerful image this evokes for us! We are the ambassadors of God's restoration and reconciliation of culture and community, churches and character, right here on this spinning sphere of Earth, life, death, and hope. It's incredibly easy to want to fix our eyes on heaven and miss out on the power we've been given to unite, restore, and reconcile—right here and right now. My pastor used to warn us of being "so heavenly bound that we're no earthly good."

We should not take this reminder lightly. But we also must be careful not to embrace it in a way that feels burdensome or obligatory, or like we have to be someone different than who we are. Jesus is a come-as-you-are Savior. He welcomes all with open arms. He extends much grace and believes that through the work of the Holy Spirit, God can get everyone to where he wants them to be. The fact that our individual journey is uniquely customized to us cannot be overstated. As many people as there ever will be, that's exactly how many different journeys there are to reconcile us to a life of freedom and oneness with God.

So many different journeys exist because each one of us is unique. Your journey to God is not the same as anyone else's. Each customized journey reflects God's incredible creativity. God knows every detail of every single person who will ever walk the face of this earth. He knows the number of hairs on your head and the unique swirl of our thumbprints. He is perfectly attuned to my unique perspective on the world, just as he has traveled each leg of your life journey with you. God knows what brings you joy and what drains me of my confidence and peace. God knows this for each one of us. On top of all this, God delights in our uniqueness, which is a direct reflection of some aspect of his character. Had he created us all the same, humanity would fail to adequately express his exponentially magnificent image.

So if God, in God's infinite wisdom, chose to create humanity with so much diversity on so many different levels and in so many different aspects, we cannot expect that we should conform to be like one another. Even—and especially—as members of the body of Christ. We should not be alarmed or perplexed when we encounter people who see things differently than we do.

Oneness is not about *conforming*. Oneness is about *transforming*.

In the body of Christ, we encounter individuals who hold wildly different perspectives from us, on a variety of different topics. Pick your topic of the day: education, politics, worship music, sexuality, climate change, race relations, security, immigration, wage equality, reproductive rights, health care, and on and on it goes. Within the body of Christ are people who support each aspect of every position. For such a very long time, I used to scratch my head in wonder over how people who claim to follow Jesus could possibly believe such-and-such about whatever it was they believed. By the same token, people have scratched their heads and wondered the same thing about me. When I mistake my position on an issue as being critical to my identity, I've let these differences stand between me and others in the body of Christ.

It's even easier to let our positions on issues divide us when we make a certain viewpoint an indicator of whether someone else is truly a believer. What a dangerous mistake to make. I am a loyal fan of the Detroit Lions. I grew up near Detroit and have fond memories of my dad taking me to football games in the Pontiac Silverdome. While you might laugh at me for my loyalty to a team that disappoints more than it delivers, I doubt you would question my Christian credentials because I'm a Lions fan. However, we often do question a person's faith when we find out what they believe about abortion or Black Lives Matter or same-sex marriage. Of course, football is not the same as these other emotionally charged issues, but I have seen some real ugliness develop between members of the body of Christ because people were on opposing sides of these conversations. It is a disheartening representation of just how far we often stray from living the oneness Jesus prayed for us.

Some of us go back and forth, wondering whether we should even engage in such conversations. When it comes to politics, some Christians say they don't discuss it. Others believe only Christians should hold public office. Still others believe political affiliation is a reflection of whether we believe rightly. As if our political affiliation is our identity. It is not. Our identity is who God sees when he looks at us—and God is not a politician.

As with every other position we hold, beyond what we've chosen to do with Jesus, our political affiliation is a marker on our faith journey. It is one way we live out our role as Christ's ambassadors. Our political affiliation (or nonaffiliation) is neither right nor wrong. It is an earthly category, plain and simple. Once we choose to follow Jesus, everything in our lives takes a back seat to that. Our affiliations and positions do not define us. Instead, they are one way in which we express our current phase of our faith journey in this particular moment. They are a reflection of the state of our hearts, the preferences of our palates, the depth of our imaginations, the breadth of our love for God and for others. There is no right answer beyond that which is motivated by love.

This kind of love is revolutionary. Michelle Alexander put it this way in an On Being conversation with Krista Tippett:

> I've been thinking a lot lately about this notion of "revolutionary love" and what that means. And it's something that I spoke with Vincent Harding quite a bit about. And I think for me what it means to be fully human is to open ourselves to fully loving one another in an unsentimental way. I'm not talking about the romantic love, or the idealized version of love, but that the simple act of caring for one another, and being aware of our connectedness as human beings, and also the reality of our suffering, and the reality that we make a lot of mistakes, and we struggle and we fail.
>
> That's all part of being human. We suffer, we love, we struggle, we fail, and then we love again. And I think trying not to imagine that we're anything more or less than that, as human beings struggling to love and find our way, making mistakes, but still yearning for a deeper connection and a sense of purpose in our lives is what being human is all about. Now of course, so many people, not just in the United States, but around the world, are struggling on a daily basis just to survive.
>
> But even among those folks, what I have found is that there's love to be found. There's joy there. There's suffering. There's redemption. All of it. And that's what it means to be human. And if we are going to evolve spiritually, morally, as human beings, we're going to lean in to caring more, and loving more for one another, and honoring our connectedness, and our oneness, and resist that impulse, that fear-driven impulse to divide and label and react with punitiveness rather than care and concern.[2]

The goal for each of us is to grow in love, not judging whether someone else is loving right or well or enough. The goal is to love—more and more. God, ourselves, our neighbor, our enemy. And we give each person grace for their journey. We understand, for example, that distilling a moment in a person's journey to categories—pro-life or pro-choice, criminal or upstanding citizen, sinner or saint—limits our ability to let God be God in the life of that person. We've been given the mandate to love—to love God and love others as we love ourselves. That, my friend, is a tall order. But this kind of love is both the breeding ground and the benefit of grace, which steps aside and makes way for God to get a person to where he wants them to be.

So if our positions, affiliations, and affinities don't identify us, what is their purpose in our lives? How might they serve as conduits for the kingdom of God, facilitating unity rather than increasing our divisions?

With this backdrop to understanding our identity and citizenship, our role as ambassadors, and the idea of affinity as a marker on a journey, we can also think about the way in which affinity gives us access to others. We can view our affinity as one way in which God targets and focuses our sphere of influence in a particular season of life. When we are clear about and secure in our citizenship in God's great kingdom and our role as ambassadors of that kingdom, our position doesn't remain as rigid as it may have been.

Some readers may be thinking this means we are waffling or being wishy-washy. These categories have to do with a person changing a position on an issue because they believe it will make them more popular or set them more firmly in the "in crowd." But this is not what we're talking about. The Bible cautions against being double-minded. That is why it behooves us to get rid of the fault lines that divide our souls. Instead, this is about being transformed by the renewing of our minds. Here again, love is our primary motivator.

During the recent presidential election, I found myself at odds with a group of people who supported a particular candidate. Despite my belief in what I've told you here, I *did* make a judgment call about the people who supported this other candidate. However, my discrimination against them was not made manifest in a questioning of their Christianity. What I found myself questioning was their particular *brand* of Christianity. Since I wasn't questioning their faith, I tricked myself into thinking I was in the clear. But the Bible challenges that perspective, telling me Christ came to tear down all the walls we build to keep one another at a distance (see Eph. 2:14). I was wrong to self-righteously distance myself from these brothers and sisters who had reached a conclusion that was different from my own. My judgment of them revealed to me an area of my life where I'd staked my identity, when my true identity is as a child of God whose citizenship is in the kingdom of God.

It was not a pretty process for me to recognize and then accept that I had been wrong. What we all need to understand is that, no matter how strongly we hold our opinions about some hot-button topics (and even not-so-hot-button topics) in our culture, there are Christians who just as strongly hold a polar opposite position. It is quite disorienting to discover that a person whose ideology, theology, or worldview we admire has a strong opinion with which we disagree. However, the more we press into this difference rather than resist it (and the person who holds that opposite viewpoint), the more we may grow to understand about God's character.

When we can press into the deeply held yet polar opposite viewpoints of our brothers and sisters in the body, we can begin to more clearly see those viewpoints as markers on a journey. These markers make way for grace—both extended and received. Why? Because these markers we uncover in the journeys of others remind us of the transformative work of the Holy Spirit in our own lives. In my lifetime, my positions and opinions about certain hot-button topics have swung from one extreme to the other. My younger self would be astounded to know where I've landed and how I'm living out my faith these days. I'm sure she would quickly build a wall between herself and me. And there's no telling what I'll think about my ninety-year-old-self when she and I meet. But life is not either/or, black and white, yes and no. We know Jesus is Truth, but anyone who says they fully understand Jesus and, by extension, Truth, should probably keep living just a little bit longer (as my grandmother used to say). There is so much we do not understand about God. Embracing the mystery of God makes way for his grace.

When we make way for more grace, we also grow in love. Isn't that the type of transformation we all seek? Pressing in rather than resisting makes it possible for me to say to my Lions-loving cohorts, when they start trash-talking those who are fans of some other team, "Oh, they're not so bad. They are football lovers, just like us." In my heart, I know those other fans may have memories of football games in a different stadium with their dad or a loyalty that's been handed down through generations or an affinity that comes as a result of their current ZIP code. I know this particular marker on their journey is no threat to my own journey. I might even believe that, one day, they'll come around and see things my way. But it's also entirely possible I may one day see things their way. Or maybe one day we will each be cheering for entirely different teams. In the meantime, when I see them sporting their jerseys and cheering for their team, I will respond with much respect. Respect for the journey. Respect for this moment in time. Much respect for the person, who was created in God's very image.

Recognizing affinity as a marker on a journey takes away our need to prove that we are right and they are wrong. It allows us to respect a different position because we respect their journey. It opens us to the idea of examining and adjusting our position as we learn from others and spend time with them. It softens us to people who see the world differently because of our growing appreciation for and relationship with them. In the interim, while we are continually being transformed, our affinity gives us a group of people to love, serve, and care for as we grow.

When I realized I was being unfair to those people who were choosing to vote for the candidate whom I didn't understand, I reached out to see if I could have a conversation with someone from that perspective. To my surprise, a few took me up on that offer. Do you know what I learned about the brothers and sisters I had maligned and sought to distance myself from? I learned they are on a journey too. Just like me. I learned they are grace-givers, and they are in need of grace. Just like me. I learned their life experiences impact the way they see the world. Just like me. I learned they are deeply, unconditionally loved by Jesus. Just like me. Just like you.

Finding the Desire to Love My Enemies

But what about when someone else's position makes it difficult for me to breathe? And what about when mine cuts off someone else's oxygen? What about terrorists? What about Hitler? What about American slave holders or modern-day human traffickers? Do they get a pass? Do we just say, "Oh, they're on a journey," as we tip our hat and say to them, "Much respect"?

No.

That is the simple answer. Evil is evil. It is the direct result of the work of our true enemy. This enemy manipulates the hearts and minds of individuals, and our societies have reaped the harvest of this evil influence. Our human nature would have us return evil for evil when we encounter it. Our instinct for self-preservation triggers our desire for revenge. But Jesus brought a surprising message to his followers when he said, "You have heard that it was said, 'Eye for eye, and tooth for tooth.' But I tell you, do not resist an evil person. If anyone slaps you on the right cheek, turn to them the other cheek also" (Matt. 5:38–39). Then, Jesus continued by saying,

> You have heard that it was said, "Love your neighbor and hate your enemy." But I tell you, love your enemies and pray for those who persecute you, that you may be children of your Father in heaven. He causes his sun to rise on the evil and the good, and sends rain on the righteous and the unrighteous. If you love those who love you, what reward will you get? Are not even the tax collectors doing that? And if you greet only your own people, what are you doing more than others? Do not even pagans do that? (Matt. 5:44–47)

So there you have it: don't resist an evil person. Love your enemies. Don't take the easy way out by loving only those who love you. Go above and beyond by extending your love to people who are not like you and those you like to hang around.

But wait a minute. It's not that easy, is it? How is anyone supposed to love like that?

Truthfully, this kind of love—sincere and transcendent—is possible only through the work of the Holy Spirit. When we live tight-fisted, holding grudges and keeping the world at arm's-length, we barricade our hearts, souls, and minds from this divine transformation. As a result, our bodies continue to repeat old habits and carry out practices that make loving our enemies impossible.

One of the most crucial ingredients of building a life that includes loving our enemies is *having a desire to love them*. What is your desire for the people in this world who have hurt your feelings, oppressed your soul, discarded your body, twisted your mind? God can redeem our thoughts toward those who have harmed or threatened us. He alone is able to cause us to live the command we've been given to love our enemies and bless those who curse us. This kind of love is supernatural. It defies convention. It heals us as we are transformed in its wake.

Psalm 37:4 reminds us to "take delight in the LORD," with a promise that he will give us the desires of our heart. In the original language, to take delight in the Lord means to be pliable before him. Each time we approach God, and as we live our lives before him, we do so with a heart that is either open to his leading or not. The more pliable our hearts, the more access we give to the Holy Spirit who, working in concert with God the Father, makes us more like Jesus. The more like Jesus we become, the more our compassion grows for those around us—even those we never thought we'd ever care about. Our desire for them begins to align with God's desire for them. God's desire is that none should perish, but that everyone would accept the gift of life that he extends to all of us. Again, the transformation begins in us first and then spills over into our interactions with the world around us. This transformation is not just a philosophical change; it can actually be measured in our bodies.

The Science of Compassion

I am constantly fascinated by the ways science confirms what God has been telling us all along. The rift between science and faith is another area that could benefit from a bit of reconciliation and oneness. One does not cancel out the other. They exist together. We live out our faith in a physical world that science helps us understand.

Science has taught us that every action has an equal and opposite reaction. Recently, a running injury landed me in the physical therapist's office. As the therapist taught me exercises to strengthen my body and retrain my brain, she explained something to me about how our bodies work. She told me that when I engage my quadriceps (the large muscle at the front of my thigh), that action turns off my hamstring muscle (the large muscle at the back of my thigh). The two muscles work in opposition to each other. The quadriceps, when engaged, allows me to extend my leg in front of me. When my hamstring is engaged, my leg bends at the knee. The two cannot work together. Either one works or the other one works. But they cannot both work at once.

A study conducted by a group of researchers at the University of Wisconsin–Madison indicates this concept holds true for the way our brain maps our emotions and our bodies' response to those emotions. Scientists have known and talked about neuroplasticity for some time. They know the brain is not stuck in a static state. It can be trained, even in adults, to respond in different ways. This is something my physical therapist is using to my advantage. The exercises my physical therapist gives me to do don't just strengthen my muscles. By having me put my body in certain positions, the goal is that my brain will get the message to tell my body to move in ways that are less likely to cause me pain when I move. In other words, my physical therapist is retraining my brain, and (thankfully) it's working.

When we see people committing evil acts, or when we receive threats to our safety from a certain person or groups of people, our brains tend to respond with defensiveness and resistance. But Jesus's teaching seems to be telling us this is the wrong response. Later, Jesus would emphasize this by telling Peter, "All who draw the sword will die by the sword" (Matt. 26:52). Someone has to de-escalate. We can't all be building better weapons while at the same time working toward oneness, unity, and peace. The two are mutually exclusive. Like the muscles in our bodies, more defensiveness works in direct opposition to oneness, unity, and peace. And, in the same way, getting closer to oneness, unity, and peace works in direct opposition to defensiveness. Compassion is one vehicle to get us there.

The researchers at the University of Wisconsin–Madison found that practicing loving-kindness and compassion actually works to create new maps in our brain. These new maps essentially "shrink" the parts of our brain that trigger our fight-or-flight response.[3] In the study, Richie Davidson, one of the researchers, defined loving-kindness and compassion by saying, "Many contemplative traditions speak of loving-kindness as the wish for happiness for others and of compassion as the wish to relieve others' suffering."[4] What is fascinating is that the change in brain patterns isn't accomplished by *making* someone happy or relieving their suffering. Instead, it's done over time by *desiring* good for the other person. As this study suggests, when we truly hope the best for others, even those who seek to harm us, in essence, it turns off our desire to want to see the other person "get what they deserve."

When we let ourselves be manipulated by rhetoric that encourages us to keep our guard up and treat others with suspicion and fear, we shut down our ability to exercise compassion. We diminish our ability to follow the teachings of Jesus, who called us to love even our enemies. Exercising loving-kindness and compassion does not excuse the evil behavior of others. In fact, I would argue a different point: extending loving-kindness and compassion toward those who would seek to harm us actually makes us aware of the influence of evil in their lives.

The enemy would like nothing more than to keep us distracted from the fact that he is the true source of all evil in the world. Even Christians forget this. We forget and then we focus our anger on *people*. Instead, we need to harness the energy of that anger and direct it toward Satan, who is at the root of every act of evil. Do not mistake the actions of people *under the influence of evil* for the *evil one*. Extending loving-kindness and compassion toward a person enables us to see more clearly the source of the evil for what it is. In the journey toward oneness—and I cannot emphasize this strongly enough—we do not wrestle against flesh and blood. If Satan can make us believe our battle is against another person or group of people, he has successfully distracted us from doing battle with him. We shout at, belittle, bomb, torture, violate, and marginalize people who are dearly loved by God when we should, instead, be waging war against Satan, our one true enemy.

When Jesus taught us to love our enemies, to bless them and pray for them, he was well aware of neuroplasticity. Jesus knew the power of compassion. He knew that *desiring good* for those we have named "enemy" can retrain our brains and transform us, through the literal renewing of our minds. Practicing loving-kindness and compassion makes it possible for us to de-escalate divisiveness and point people toward something more.

SIX

AWAKE IN THE DARK

On August 9, 2014, in Ferguson, Missouri, Officer Darren Wilson and Michael Brown, an eighteen-year-old male, had what some might call an altercation. Many accounts have surfaced as to how the events unfolded that afternoon, but in the end, Michael Brown was dead and his body lay face down in the middle of the street. There was no doubt as to how Michael Brown died; he died because Officer Darren Wilson discharged his gun and the bullets landed in Michael Brown's body.

Michael Brown did not have a weapon in his possession. Later reports would indicate that Brown had stolen a box of cigars from a local convenience store. Some witnesses stated that when Brown was confronted by Wilson, he put his hands in the air. Some say he charged Officer Wilson. Later, reports from the Department of Justice would reveal these accounts to be untrue.[1] Officer Wilson told investigators that Michael Brown reached into the car for the officer's gun. After he fell to the ground, Michael Brown's body lay in the street for hours. His death fanned the flames of a smoldering and growing movement against the deaths of young, unarmed men and women of color in America.

The stories being reported in the news raised questions of police brutality and abuse of power. In case after case, the white person (often a police officer) responsible for the death of an unarmed person of color was not indicted. In case after case, the white person went free.

Reactions to the death of Michael Brown are sharply divided. Many who support Michael Brown call for changes to corrupt policing policies and judicial systems. Supporters of Michael Brown and their allies are frustrated by systems that have worked to marginalize entire groups of people for as long as they can remember. Rising up out of the ashes of the deaths of people like Michael Brown, Trayvon Martin, Eric Garner, Sandra Bland, Tamir Rice, Renisha McBride, and so many more, people took to the streets and organized themselves and became a movement with a mantra that proclaims, "Black Lives Matter."

People who support and sympathize with Officer Wilson are often white and/or members of, or loyal to, law enforcement and the systems it represents. They are frustrated by a changing demographic and a culture that threatens to shift the power to something no one has ever seen before. They feel as if their rights are being stripped away and that they constantly have to walk on eggshells for fear of being called racist or politically incorrect. They hear the chants of "Black Lives Matter" and often respond in all sincerity with an edited version of that mantra: "All Lives Matter."

But many in the Black Lives Matter movement feel they have been edited out for far too long. They are weary of being told how to behave, how to protest, and what tone to use when they do. And then, after all is said and done—after they have done exactly as they've been told to do, especially during encounters with those in authority over them—it seems there is still no chance of actually getting home safely, if getting home happens at all. To hear "Black Lives Matter" edited adds fuel to an already growing fire.

Officer Wilson admitted he killed Michael Brown. There was never any dispute about that fact. What was in question was whether Officer Wilson feared for his life and, in this case, a grand jury decided the officer did, indeed, fear his life was in danger when he shot Michael Brown. In the wake of the continually breaking news, tension mounted and rioting ensued in Ferguson. From my home in Nebraska, the media was all I had to tell me what was going on. The news media. Social media. Print media. All of it was someone else's perspective and someone else's account of what was actually going on.

I share this with you in an attempt to provide context. Others have written far more eloquently than I about the history, social structures, systems, and powers at play in Ferguson. I'm not here to break it down and explain why it went down the way it did. What I want to share with you is my experience of the event. All a person can ever really tell is his or her own story, right?

What I know is that I had to go to Ferguson to see it for myself.

Here's what I tell people about my trip to Ferguson: First, I tell them I was compelled to go there. I also tell them that the logistics of getting me there were nothing short of miraculous. I tell them about how oppressively hot it was and that I was sweaty, sticky, and stinky the entire time I was there. I tell them how I stood on the street where Michael Brown died and how his blood still stained the ground. I tell them how there was no relief from the heat because everywhere we went the air-conditioning was broken. I tell them how the heat served as a depressing metaphor for the situation at hand.

These are the things I talk about when people ask me about my trip to Ferguson that August after Officer Darren Wilson shot Michael Brown and Michael Brown died in the street. Of course, there are parts of the story I don't share with everyone, and I don't share them often. They are not easy thoughts to offer up, and it may be true that they are still unfolding.

We each have a certain investment in the status quo. We know our roles, we play our parts, and we can sleepwalk our way through it. Have you ever encountered a sleepwalker?

One night, when my son was in middle school, my husband and I were asleep in our bed. It was the middle of the night—maybe two or three o'clock in the morning. I am a sound sleeper, but that night, in my dreams, I heard my son say loudly, "Bye, Mom!" Only, I knew it wasn't a dream.

I woke up and looked in my son's room, but he wasn't there. I could hear sounds coming from downstairs, so I made my way down the steps, and there was my son. He was wearing pajamas, but with one hand against the wall for balance, he was working to get his feet into his sneakers. One foot after the other, he stepped into the shoes with the basketball pump sewn into the tongue.

"Where are you going?" I asked him.

"I have to go get my stuff," he answered.

"What stuff?" I asked. "Where is it?"

"My stuff," he answered. "It's at the school."

He didn't look directly at me, but in that moment, I knew he was asleep. He was sleepwalking and completely unaware he was standing in the foyer, sneakers on his feet, and one hand now on the doorknob. He looked awake, but his behavior and his words were a dead giveaway that he was not. This was my first and only experience with a sleepwalker. Up to that moment, I had imagined sleepwalkers shuffling around with a glazed look in their eyes, their arms outstretched in front of them. In other words, I was sure a sleepwalker would be easy to identify, even from a distance. All I knew about sleepwalkers was that they should not be awakened. From what I remembered about what I'd heard, waking a sleepwalker could be a traumatic experience, for both the one doing the waking and the one being awakened.

That night my son suddenly changed course. On his own, he turned around, went back upstairs, and from that spot in the foyer I watched him turn toward his bedroom. By the time I climbed the steps and peeked into his room, he was back in his bed, fast asleep. In the morning, he had no memory of what had transpired that night, and he never walked around in his sleep again. But I learned a person can look like they're awake, when really, they aren't.

I don't know if what I've heard about waking up a sleepwalker is true. What I know is that, in Ferguson, I began to feel as if parts of me were waking up to perspectives and truths I'd never realized before. Some of these revelations have been difficult for me to process, while others have been easier to absorb.

What I know for sure is that God is madly in love with Michael Brown, the young black man who was killed that afternoon. I think that's important to understand. I am also convinced that God is madly in love with Officer Darren Wilson, the white police officer who shot and killed Michael Brown.

That too is important to understand. I am confident God takes great delight in the people who rioted in Ferguson in the aftermath of both the shooting and the subsequent court decision that Officer Wilson would go free. God also takes great delight in the people who raised money for the Brown family, as well as those who raised money for the Wilson family. God does not delight in these people because of their actions. He delights in them—and in us—despite their actions and in the midst of their actions. When we are at our best, and even when we are at our worst, God is rooting for us. For *us*. Not for our cause, as if one were right and the other wrong. God is rooting for *us*, giving us the opportunity to learn more about love and grace, and what it means to forgive, to grieve, to lament, and to heal.

God is the president of our fan club. When our hearts are broken and burdened under the unrelenting heat of oppression, the devastating loss of life, and the kind of fear that blinds us to reason and Third Way alternatives, God weeps right along with us. God meets us in the oppressive heat of our very own Ferguson, where he is the only one who knows the entire truth.

It is dangerous to let ourselves get away with sleepwalking our way through life, especially when we are children of the Light. We cannot sleepwalk our way through or around the injustices and the oppressions of this world. When we close our eyes or refuse to listen; when we pit ourselves against the one who cries out from the side of the road, we are carrying on the tradition of those who passed right by the one who had been beaten, robbed, and left for dead in the story of the good Samaritan. The image of God is not honored; he is not glorified when we exit. God is not a God of "out." He is the God of "through." God enters into our wilderness experiences. He walks through the valley of the shadow of death right along with us. God is our ever-present help *in* trouble. God is our shelter *in* a storm. We are quick to whisper or cry out, "Come quickly, Lord Jesus!" but let's not get confused and hope our best choice is to get *out* of an uncomfortable or trying situation. As I once heard a preacher say, "You don't get to be raptured away from me." God is an expert at taking us through a trial—and making us better because of it. As disciples of Christ, we are challenged to follow his lead. When we learn about unjust systems and communities and people in danger, that is our invitation to wake up, roll up our sleeves, and enter in as ambassadors of reconciliation and children of Light. When we show up, filled to overflowing with the Holy Spirit, we illuminate the darkness and expose injustice wherever it has rooted itself and gained ground.

The answer the world gives us to the problem of injustice is to choose a side and, once we've done that, to find our identity in that particular side of the argument. Anyone who sees things differently isn't worth our time, according to the way the world operates. We make the argument our priority, and if we are not careful, the people for whom we claim to be advocating get lost in the shuffle. Even a good cause can leave people out or lead us to judge those who don't understand, who don't see things the way we do. Even a passion for unity and oneness can be misguided when it insists on unity and oneness looking a certain way. When the people on the other side of our argument become our enemies, and we identify them as such, we have let our argument become our idol.

Ultimately, it is the darkness I fight against. Not you. Not even those who would call themselves my enemy. The darkness is sneaky though. It wraps itself around me and I get comfortable with the way it rests on my shoulders. We don't even notice the way it hinders our vision. We stop caring about the fact that we can't see past our hands anymore. Evil masquerades in darkness. Before we know it, we've given in to it. We are lulled to sleep, even though we look like we are wide awake. We even fool ourselves. Paul reminds us of this when he writes, "For you were once darkness, but now you are light in the Lord. Live as children of light. . . . Everything exposed by the light becomes visible—and everything that is illuminated becomes a light. . . . This is why it is said: 'Wake up, sleeper, rise from the dead, and Christ will shine on you'" (Eph. 5:8, 13–14).

Oppression, injustice, long-standing grudges, and hatred are types of darkness against which we can take a stand. But we've got to be awake to recognize them. These systems and practices entrap and entangle and threaten to strangle, in much the same way the heat in Ferguson pressed down around the small group I was with. People who feel as if they are sweltering beneath the heat of oppression will try to tell you how they feel. It doesn't matter if we agree that they are sweltering, especially if we're driving by in our climate-controlled vehicles or watching on our giant televisions from our living rooms. People who tell us repeatedly that they are being oppressed deserve to have others sit up and take notice. They deserve to have some of us so-called Jesus-followers listen to their stories and shine some light on their situation. And we are obligated to do so.

The heat in Ferguson followed us everywhere. We'd spot a restaurant and head inside, only to be told the AC was out of order. On the day we went to church to worship, we were sure we'd find relief from the heat. Instead, we were greeted by box fans that churned against any hope of stirring up a cool breeze inside the packed sanctuary. The preacher, Reverend

F. Willis Johnson, told us they'd had the AC fixed the day before, in anticipation of a large crowd that Sunday. It was no use, the preacher said. "The Freon," he told us, "has freed itself and moved on from here." So we slid into pews and folding chairs and let our hot shoulders, arms, hips, and legs press up against complete strangers and dear friends. We waved our bulletins in thwarted attempts at pushing back against the oppression of the heat.

No matter what we tried, we could not escape the triple-digit heat and its equally sweltering humidity. Our discomfort was an incessant reminder of the truth that people all over the world live in deplorable, stifling, rank, and crushing situations of oppression. This oppression is the direct result of policies and perspectives that depend on a world in which "us vs. them" is the norm, and everyone sleepwalks through the role they've been given to play in the saga. "Us vs. them" can look like phobias and -isms, but it can also look like religion.

What a breath of fresh air it is to see people waking up from their sleep, recognizing that Christ did, indeed, die for all. No exceptions. He does not blame us or shame us or pit us against one another. He does not turn the channel when our circumstances make him uncomfortable. He doesn't dream of being raptured or air-lifted out of a culture that needs every ounce of hope, love, and grace that the Spirit of God, through the people of God, can pour into it.

I am a black woman living in America. Recently I was walking down the street near a country club in our neighborhood and three young white men yelled unmentionable things to me through the rolled-down windows of their car. They were wrong. Juvenile, at best. At worst, they were racist, profane, and misogynistic. But they kept driving. They did not turn around and stop their car in front of me. They did not touch me or threaten me or wield some sort of perverted power over me. They did not discharge a weapon and violate my body. I got home safely. At least my body did.

When reviewed from a purely physical perspective, my experience that afternoon, and others like it, was "light and momentary." As you may have guessed, this was far from my first experience of that kind. But I'm writing about it, aren't I? Because whatever people may say about names that never hurt us, words, it turns out, have power.

If we're being honest, it's hard to separate the body from what goes on in the soul, right? In fact, we've already talked about how important it is to keep a single-mindedness about us, so that our hearts, minds, souls, and bodies are treated as a whole as we each allow God to do the work of reconciling us to ourselves. And so imagine the damage done to those who experience compounded anxiety, depression, marginalization, and oppression every moment of every day. Consider the United States' mass incarceration situation. Think about the sex- and human-trafficking industry. Read about the inequities that run rampant in public school districts in poor communities. Take note of the rise in "despair deaths" among middle-aged, white Americans who are increasingly succumbing to suicide, drug overdose, and liver disease associated with alcohol use.[2] Remember that every single person in those situations is a person God loves exponentially.

We Are All Valedictorians

Sometimes I hear people try to rationalize their indifference to these situations by blaming those trapped in systems of oppression or addiction for the choices they have made. The truth is, you and I have made choices too. We are all criminals. Every single one of us. We disregard the speed limit. We fail to pay our traffic fines. We drive while intoxicated. We smoke(d) weed and snort(ed) cocaine (back in college). We drank beer before we were legally old enough to do so. We sexually harassed a former co-worker. These things and more—soliciting a prostitute, shoplifting a candy bar, breaking and entering, vandalizing, that pen in your pocket that belongs to your employer—they are all crimes. And if we don't find our particular variety on this list, that doesn't make us exempt. Because all of us are sinners.

We do not sin on a bell curve. When it comes to sinning, we are each a valedictorian. And just as we take the image of God with us into our workplaces, marketplaces, gathering places, and worship places, we carry our sinful, criminal selves there as well. It behooves us to acknowledge this. Not because we should wallow in our shortcomings, but so that we can identify with the people whose shortcomings seem so much more horrendous than our own. They are not. We are just like them. All of us.

I've heard people say the thing we hate the most in someone else is the very same thing we hate in ourselves. What if that's true? What if we are all the same after all? What if we are, at the same time, us *and* them?

The truth is that we are both. We are people who love deeply, serve freely, and give generously. We weep with those who weep and rejoice with those who rejoice. We are empathetic, sympathetic, and compassionate. And we are also inherently geared toward self-preservation. Most of the time, we make it through a day without these two parts of ourselves ganging up on us. But sometimes our instinct for survival wants to make sure we know it's still there. It is a difficult instinct to combat. This desire to protect ourselves and those we love is innate. It is wired into our DNA and programmed into our brains.

A lot of the time, the only thing that separates me and you from the people our society has labeled *criminal* is the fact that we didn't get caught. Or, if we did get caught, we found ourselves beneficiaries of a corrupt system that worked in our favor. You and I? We are criminals too. In this we are all, truly, the same. We are criminals, and God loves us.

The Appropriateness of Lament

I was in Ferguson for three days, and on two of those days, I stood on the street where Michael Brown was shot. The first time I stood there was a Friday afternoon, and the atmosphere was somber. A shrine of stuffed animals, balloons, and roses had taken shape on the dotted yellow line that ran down the center of the street. A few people stood by, talking in hushed voices. Every now and then, someone would walk over to the memorial and stand there—head bowed, hands folded.

The next time I visited was Saturday afternoon. Our little group returned to that street, but to quite a different scene. On Saturday, the street was mobbed with people. The atmosphere was more like a carnival. People took selfies in front of the shrine. Groups of people wearing matching T-shirts passed out fliers. Like me, hardly anyone there that Saturday afternoon was actually *from* Ferguson. Each time I asked someone, "Where are you from?" they told me they'd traveled to get to this place, just like me.

Despite this fact, and also despite the fact that we were all on a street just like yours, where an entire community of people lives and sleeps and makes love and cooks dinner and drinks wine and helps their children with homework and argues with their lover and pays bills and goes to work, the street and its neighborhood had become a spectacle. Cars drove slowly down the street as pedestrians weaved between the vehicles. It was hard to know why we were all there. I mean, we were there because one person had shot and killed another person. That much we knew. That much was clear. But we each brought our own stories with us too.

Some of us were there because a police officer was being criticized for defending himself.

Some of us were there because a black man had been killed.

Some of us were there because a white police officer shot and killed an unarmed black man.

Some of us were there because we knew what it was like to take a life.

Some of us were there because we knew what it was like to lose a son.

People had other reasons too. Probably as many reasons as there were people.

On that street, that Saturday, two different groups of people had set up enormous speakers and were blasting music into the air. On the eastern end of the street, in front of the apartment buildings that helped make up this community, were a group of people whose music sounded a call that had become so very familiar in the heat of frustration, defeat, and hopelessness. "F— the police!" the lyrics pounded out from the speakers. I stood on the sidewalk and felt the bass pounding in my chest.

On the western end of that same street, in an open space covered with grass and shaded by mature, leafy trees, a church group had erected a stage with mammoth speakers pointed toward the crowd. A hip-hop gospel vibe thumped at me where I stood, and over and over again in the middle of my chest, the sounds of the praise team's Jesus songs collided with the profanity of the other music. I didn't realize it yet, but I was witnessing lamenting, on an oppressively hot summer day, in the middle of an all-American street, in a place called Ferguson, Missouri. In the moment, they both seemed pointless to me. Clanging cymbals. Tone-deaf gongs.

From where I stood—all hot, sweaty, stinky, and mad—there seemed to be no hope in either message. What I saw was two groups, completely oblivious to one another, pounding out a message, both of which were loud and unrelenting. Neither one got through to the other.

Standing there, I shook my head and fought the urge to feel hopeless and agitated. I swallowed down the desire to shout out to everyone, "Can we all just shut up for a minute, please?" I didn't say it, but I was thinking it. It was my own lament.

Lamenting doesn't really seem to be doing much good while one is doing it. A lament is chaotic and messy. A lament is loud and wailing. A lament is confused and confusing. While lamenting, we're focused on our need to express the despair, grief, fear, or deep sense of loss and pain that has settled itself in our souls. It doesn't look pretty, and it isn't organized. It doesn't conform to any standards or particular social mores. An individual lament serves us, and only us. It is a working out of a deep despair. It is a release of emotions. It is loud and unrelenting. But it might also be quietly steady and mournful, releasing itself in moans and agonizing sighs of emptiness. The prophets lamented in ashes and sackcloth. Today, we lament through musical vibes that crash into one another, protests that block streets, fists raised in the air, and signs held overhead at rallies and conventions. We lament in living rooms with the blinds closed, our tears falling silently onto the carpet.

A lament may not look as if it's doing anything important and may be inconvenient for those who cross its path. But it is paving the way for restoration and reconciliation in places we cannot see. We are wrong to tell a person they can't or shouldn't lament. We are wrong to tell a person they should lament in a certain way. We are wrong when we tell people their lamentation is inappropriate. It is not okay to tell someone they shouldn't be angry or mad.

I stood on that sidewalk with the disparate musical selection beating me down, and I wondered what it would take to pull the plug on all the noise. I wanted to know what it would take for the Jesus people and the people who were angry at the police to turn this whole thing into something less than a spectacle. Less than a carnival. Less than shouting at one another from different ends of a street in someone else's neighborhood. A neighborhood, by the way, that might need some space to breathe. A neighborhood that might want some time to grieve. A neighborhood that might appreciate an atmosphere in which its people could gather their thoughts and discover exactly how they feel about things for themselves.

The truth, though, is that all of it was grief. It wasn't time for coming together. Not yet. In that moment, all of it was one monstrous, heart-wrenching demonstration of the effects of oppression, loss, anger, and being silenced and marginalized. Lament looks like all of this. It looks like "F— the police!" and it looks like gospel music on a portable stage, and it looks like everything in between. We all felt the grief, and the heat intensified our lament.

Look and See

Five of us took this trip to Ferguson together. That Saturday, for about thirty minutes in the carnival atmosphere, we lost one another in the crowd. Weaving in and out between the bodies, our small group got separated and we each have our very own stories about what that was like. This is how I came to be standing, all by myself, in the middle of the crazy crashing of humanity. Through the noise and press of bodies, my eyes caught a glimpse of something. Only, it wasn't some*thing*. He was some*body*. A little boy, maybe five years old. His shirt was off. He wore his caramel skin and his chocolate curls without a care in the world. He had no idea these features might one day put him at a disadvantage. He cartwheeled and ran about as five-year-olds are prone to do. He laughed and smiled and seemed completely oblivious to the heat or the clash of cultures or the lament in the air.

I had so many thoughts about that little boy. And my mind wandered back to the night before. The night we'd stood quietly on this same street. When we first arrived on that street, my friend Jennifer walked right up to a group of men, all in short-sleeved, khaki-colored, button-down shirts with collars. Their pants were loose fitting and made of the same cotton and khaki-colored fabric as their shirts. Some of the men wore knitted caps on their heads, and they stood beneath a tree. They were clearly at their post, keeping watch on that street and over the makeshift memorial in the middle of the road. Their presence spoke volumes, even though they stood silently or spoke in soft voices to one another.

When she stood beneath the tree, engaged in friendly conversation with these men, Jennifer seemed completely upbeat and relaxed. Everyone laughed and smiled, and the gentlemen in khaki outfits offered kindness and respectful dialogue about how it is they thought it had come to this—another unarmed black man (boy?) shot dead by a white police officer. ("This is America," they answered.) *What needed to happen to make it stop?* ("Where are your churches and your preachers?" they asked in return.) *How much longer could it keep happening before something burst wide open and all hell broke loose?* ("Not very," they said.)

When would it change for this little boy? When would it start to matter for him that his brown skin and his curled hair might make him a liability? I'd raised a son just like him. We had given our son *the talk.* When (not if) a police officer stops you, we had told him, be polite. Be respectful. It's a universal message, especially for people raising boys. "Get home safely." That is the goal. Keep your hands in full view. Don't make any sudden moves. Say, "Yes, sir," or "Yes, ma'am." Take off your hood when you enter a store. Don't carry a backpack into a store with you. Look the clerk/officer/teacher in the eye and be respectful. Get home safely. Say, "The registration is in the glove box. May I reach over and get it, officer?" When would this little boy hear those directives from the people who simply wanted him to get home safely? Or had he already heard them?

From the corner of my eye, I saw that Jennifer—the same friend who'd walked up to the khaki-clad men the night before—had also caught sight of this little boy. She snapped a few pictures with her camera, and we both let his delight wash over us in the blistering heat. We moved closer to each other and remarked about the little boy's cuteness and carefree bliss. Our other friends found us there, and we agreed we'd all seen and heard enough. There was nothing more we could do, so we made our way to the parking lot beside one of the buildings in the apartment complex and piled into our rented vehicle.

In silence, we snaked our way out of the neighborhood, past the loudspeakers, matching T-shirts, and crowds of people from everywhere but Ferguson. We needed to decompress. We looked for a restaurant but ended up parking in a vacant lot. In that stolen moment that included air-conditioning and the leather seats of the inside of a rented SUV, Jennifer put words to her grief. In another lifetime, nearly three decades before, she had been a journalist. She had interviewed countless people from all walks of life.

Jennifer sat in the backseat and told us, through her tears, that she could take some of her news stories from twenty-five years before, change the names and the dates, and republish them today. They'd still be good, she said. The blood. The shooting. The division. The anger. The fear. The oppression. Recently, I asked Jennifer about that moment. This is what she said:

> I remember very specifically the feeling and then having a conversation about it. We were sitting in that parking lot, and I just broke down in tears. I was so sad, and I was so mad, and it just felt exactly like stories I had written twenty-five years earlier. Just change the dates on them.
>
> You know, since it's not a story that I have to live every day, I could just completely turn my back on all that. I could really go years with just assuming that everything I'm hearing ("It's getting better! It's getting better! See, we've elected Barack Obama!"), as well as all the other lists of things that people offer to show that there's been some kind of progress made. To get to a place where you're confronted to take off the Band-Aid and look at the unhealed wound underneath was very eye-opening for me, and very important for me.

I think it's important for everybody to figure out how to put themselves in that kind of position. White people like me could never live that story, but I think we have got to look at that story and look at the really hard parts of it.

For me, the most shocking part is what I said in that parking lot: it's just a change of dates. That just feels so hopeless in some ways. But yet, in other ways, if more of us would acknowledge it, then maybe that isn't hopeless. Acknowledging it helps us see it. And anytime we see something, there is automatically hope there. Because when we see things, we're saying, "This is real," and we have to look. When you look and see something, you have to do something.

Jonathan Brooks leads Canaan Community Church on Chicago's South Side. In a conversation on the *Quick to Listen* podcast, he spoke about Jesus turning over the tables in the temple. "The following sentence after he flips over the money changers' tables is not, 'Oh. I went overboard.' It's 'Good, now there is room for the crippled and the lame so that I can heal them.'"[3] Our love for others should lead us to action, and the purpose of that action is to make room for those at the margins so they can get to God.

I pray our young black men and our police officers, and everyone else you and I can think of, always make it home safely. I pray the body of Christ can gather together and speak into the darkness with one voice. I pray we will plead with God *and* protest, love *and* lament. I pray we will work to turn over the tables of injustice that block a direct path to God. And I pray we do all of this as worship, acknowledging that without God, we can do nothing.

SEVEN

OUR BREAKING POINT

One day not too long ago, a woman from our church was working in a kitchen. A pot of soup simmered on the stove, and as the soup simmered, this woman held a bowl just above the pot. She'd done this before, hoping to minimize the risk of soup dripping across the stovetop as she ladled it from the pot into the waiting bowl. But this time, the bowl slipped from her hand and landed in the pot of simmering soup. When the bowl connected with the hot liquid in the pot, the bowl exploded, sending extremely hot soup flying in every direction. Much of the hot soup landed on the woman's arm and face, with disastrous results. Suffering from third-degree burns, the woman was rushed to a hospital, where medical experts tended to her injuries.

The phenomenon that causes glass to break when subjected to a sudden change in temperature is called thermal shock. When glass is heated unevenly, the hot glass expands. The unheated glass remains the same. As a result of the uneven expansion, the glass undergoes a great amount of stress. This stress often results in broken glass. My grandfather taught me about this when I was a teenager.

After my grandmother passed away, my grandfather came to live with us. He'd sit on the banquette in our kitchen, one leg crossed over the other, his right hand resting on our butcher-block table. Sometimes I'd pass through the kitchen on my way to somewhere else. Other times, I'd stand at the counter for a bit to talk with him. I often made him sardine sandwiches on white bread with mustard. One afternoon, after I'd made the sandwich, I reached into the dishwasher to get a glass for some ice water. The dishwasher had just finished its cycle, so the glass in my hand was warm. Sitting at the kitchen table, my grandfather watched me from beneath his eyebrows. "That glass is going to break," he said to me as I dropped a few ice cubes into the glass. "No, it won't," I replied, with unfounded confidence. Holding the glass in my hand, I turned on the tap at the kitchen sink and positioned the glass beneath a stream of cold water. Looking back, I imagine my grandfather silently counting beneath his breath, "One, two . . ." *Bam!* Just as he'd predicted, the glass formed a deep crack, right there in my hand. The glass held together, but it was no longer good for a glass of water.

I think, for a lot of us, the journey toward oneness and unity often feels like thermal shock to our souls and our hearts. The stress of the work often feels like uneven pressure, causing us to shatter under the weight of it all. Sometimes it's not even the oneness journey that breaks us. Sometimes the simple act of living through a regular day in our particular corner of this broken world creates its own brand of thermal shock in our lives. Sometimes we break like the glass I held in my hand that day, without any collateral damage. Other times, we explode, just like that bowl that dropped in the pot of hot soup. Not only do we break, but we cause immense pain and damage to those around us.

Our Brokenness Is God's Way In

We are brokenhearted people. Much has been said about the state of our brokenness, and I must admit, I have grown weary of our claim to being broken and messy. Even so, we have been, indeed. But sometimes we get sloppy and wear our brokenness as a badge of honor, or we invoke our messiness as a reason for staying that way.

Consider this tale, a gift from the Hassidic tradition and recounted by Parker J. Palmer in his book *Healing the Heart of Democracy*:

> A disciple asks the rebbe: "Why does the Torah tell us to 'place these words upon your hearts'? Why does it not tell us to place these holy words in our hearts?" The rebbe answers: "It is because as we are, our hearts are closed, and we cannot place the holy words in our hearts. So we place them on top of our hearts. And there they stay until, one day, the heart breaks and words fall in."[1]

If God is going to get through to us, it's often through our brokenness. He makes his way in because of our brokenness. Through our brokenness—despite our brokenness—God transforms us. Nothing is beyond God's capacity, ability, or desire to redeem, restore, and reconcile. This journey has no timetable. Some tragic heartbreaks make restoration and reconciliation seem impossible and even undesirable. But reconciliation is God's gift to us, and to the human condition, even though it sometimes arrives through the pain of a broken heart.

Bryan Stevenson is the author of *Just Mercy* and the founder of the Equal Justice Initiative (EJI). EJI is "a legal practice dedicated to defending the poor, the wrongly condemned, and those trapped in the furthest reaches of our criminal justice system."[2] *Just Mercy* focuses on the story of Walter McMillian, a man convicted and sentenced to die for a murder he did not commit. As he tells us the story of Walter McMillian, Stevenson does a masterful job weaving in stories of others who also have been wrongly incarcerated and trapped in an arguably corrupt system that too few of us are informed enough about on any given day.

Day after day, Stevenson and his team at EJI encounter and seek to make right the inhumane and unjustifiably harsh conditions so many prisoners endure. The work that Stevenson and his team do on behalf of others is truly heartbreaking. It leaves a mark. Day after day, working on behalf of the wrongly convicted, forming a bond of trust with them, and far too often seeing their life cut unjustifiably short via lethal injection or the electric chair takes its toll on a person. Stevenson writes, "You can't effectively fight abusive power, poverty, inequality, illness, oppression, or injustice and not be broken by it. We are all broken by something."[3]

The Word of God makes it clear that we are in desperate need of a Savior and that we fail miserably when left to our own devices. In John 15, Jesus reminds us we are not the ones in charge:

> Remain in me, as I also remain in you. No branch can bear fruit by itself; it must remain in the vine. Neither can you bear fruit unless you remain in me.
>
> I am the vine; you are the branches. If you remain in me and I in you, you will bear much fruit; *apart from me you can*

do nothing. If you do not remain in me, you are like a branch that is thrown away and withers; such branches are picked up, thrown into the fire and burned. (John 15:4–6, emphasis mine)

We are helpless without the presence of Christ in us. It's true. But it is precisely the presence of Christ in us, through the power of the Holy Spirit, that changes everything. We are sinners, yes. But we are also saved. We are microcosms of God's great work in the cosmos. The work God is doing on a grand scale to restore the world to itself and to God is also happening on a smaller scale in each of us who invites God to take the lead in the way we live our lives.

Eclipsing the World

Imagine this: You've got two disks in your hand. They can be whatever you want them to be. Two plates, two Frisbees, two coins, two round pieces of cardboard. Now, imagine you're holding one disk in your right hand and the other in your left hand. Pretend the disk in your left hand represents the kingdom of God, while the one in your right hand represents the kingdom of this world.

At the foundation of the world, when God spoke all things into existence and before sin entered the world, there was complete harmony between humanity and God. Our relationship with God in the beginning can be represented by one single disk—the one in your left hand. But then sin showed up on the scene and we *broke off* our relationship with God. I think it's important to remember that we chose to end the relationship—not God. Our choice was an invitation for brokenness to take up residence in us. In that moment, we chose to go our own way. Our decision infused disharmony and dissonance into the relationship we had with God, and so we were shut out from the Garden of Eden; we became refugees from paradise and immigrants in the kingdom of this world. But our choice also infused disharmony and dissonance into our relationhip with one another, with Adam quickly throwing Eve under the bus, along with God: "The woman you put here with me," he said (Gen. 3:12). That second disk—the one in your right hand—represents the kingdom of this world and is the kingdom we chose instead, when we disobeyed God and followed our own path instead of his.

Now, imagine you are holding those two disks in your hands, far away from one another, and imagine God on the left and us on the right. We, as they say, are far from God, indeed. But from the moment we chose the kingdom of this world, God has been at work to bring us back to him—to reconcile the world and its cities, communities, and people back to himself. To heal our brokenness, in all of the places it snakes its way into our lives.

This reconciliation story plays out every single day and in every single moment of each day. As individuals, we choose our way over God's ways, over and over again. We cheat on our taxes. We gossip. We lie. We steal. We sleep with the wrong person. We murder someone's character, and we also commit physical murder. We party too much. We keep too much. We spend too much. We work too much. We can't help it. We are sinners. But we are also being transformed. We are being saved. We are being made new, despite our bent toward wrongdoing. As we give more and more control of our lives to God, we become more and more like his Son, Jesus. Only when we experience this mysterious transformation can we pretend to begin to understand it. It defies all reason and isn't logical.

But slowly, over time, the person being transformed starts to notice something different, and so do the people around her. This is God, reconciling us—one by one—to himself.

Again, we are reminded that the arc of the story of God reconciling the world to himself is much longer than the arc of our individual stories of reconciliation to God. It is the single arc of time itself, and we are players in the greatest story ever told. We are ambassadors. We are the unlikely revolutionaries. We are salt, and we are light, set on a hill.

So back to those two disks you're holding.

Slowly begin to slide the disk representing the kingdom of God over the surface of the disk that represents the kingdom of this world. Keep the disk in your right hand slightly behind the one in your left, so that the kingdom of God eclipses the kingdom of this world. As you allow the kingdom of God to make its way over the top of the disk in your right hand, pay attention to the section where the two discs overlap. Now, imagine yourself—along with all the rest of us—living out life, right there in the space of the overlap. Right there is where we find ourselves. Right there is where we're living out the revolution—in our communities, in our churches, and in our relationships with God, one another, and our own souls.

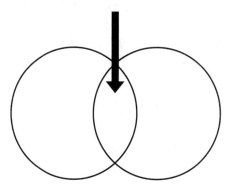

Broken Open

It is true that we are broken. And that makes things messy. But brokenness is only part of the journey. The trap we often fall into is, as Bryan Stevenson puts it, our "comfort level with reducing people to their worst act and acting in very extreme, harsh, punitive ways."[4] We are not the worst thing we have ever done. Neither is anyone else. Our brokenness is not the totality of who we are, and when we can find a way to see it, our brokenness is also a gift.

When we invest ourselves—in our communities, our families, our churches, our relationships—brokenness is part of the journey. This kind of brokenness is what that Hassidic tale points us toward. Parker Palmer says it this way:

> If you hold your knowledge of self and world wholeheartedly, your heart will at times get broken by loss, failure, defeat, betrayal, or death. What happens next in you and the world around you depends on *how* your heart breaks. If it breaks *apart* into a thousand pieces, the result may be anger, depression, and disengagement. If it breaks *open* into greater capacity to hold the complexities and contradictions of human experience, the result may be new life.[5]

And so let's reconsider our talk of brokenness. Let's hold it up to the Light and consider whether we've been broken *open* or *apart* by this life and the world in which we're living. When thinking of it this way, it's easier to see how our systems often end up being forces for destruction and pain, hurling broken shards of power and pride at those who happen to find themselves holding the short straw. The same is true for relationships that break our hearts. These experiences can make us or break us, as they say. As ambassadors of the kingdom of God and agents of reconciliation, we are invited by God to boldly present our heartbreak to him and let him transform it so that even our broken hearts become conduits for wholeness, in some crazily mysterious metamorphosis of grace and hope.

Bryan Stevenson says,

> There is a strength, a power even, in understanding broken-ness, because embracing our brokenness creates a need and desire for mercy, and perhaps a corresponding need to show mercy. When you experience mercy, you learn things that are hard to learn otherwise. You see things you can't otherwise see; you hear things you can't otherwise hear. You begin to recognize the humanity that resides in each of us.[6]

Regaining Focus

All around us, people have gotten bold in their denunciations of one another. We have grown brave in our dismissals of another person's story. We have become experts at driving a wedge instead of building a bridge. Whether the topic is race, sexual orientation, abortion, global warming, terrorism, or immigration, it really doesn't matter. Our collective language has grown vitriolic. We are drowning in our fear of the future, dislike of our neighbors, an affinity for comfort, a general distrust, and a tragic loss of hope.

If we're not careful, we might get caught up in the fallout. We might lose focus and feel our feet start to slip. What does that look like? How does it feel? It looks like throwing in the towel or taking sides or trying to exact revenge. It feels like worry, doubt, and hopelessness. It manipulates anger and fear, and it manifests in abusive power and marginalization. If we let it simmer, it starts to look, feel, act, and sound a lot like hate.

The language we use when we talk about others, and about ourselves, correlates directly to the condition of our hearts. If there is division in our hearts, our language will perpetuate division in our culture and in the world around us. If we are experiencing a breach in our relationship with God or ourselves, or both, that breach will show up in the impact of our words in the world. When we allow the world around us to divide our attention and distract us from believing in the power of God to overcome evil, we surrender our faith to the storm. This is the true danger of brokenness. When the world—with its worries, fears, grief, and strife—presses in on us, we can succumb to the impulse to look away from God, instead of toward him. The true danger of brokenness is that we allow it to keep us, even lead us, away from God, from others, and from ourselves.

This is the difference between being broken open and being broken apart. In your own life, have your heartbreaks and disappointments served as an open door or a dividing wall? We needn't be hard on ourselves when we realize our hurts have made us bitter and our bitterness has made us divisive. This is natural. Additionally, depending on the size of the hurt or the source of our pain, our journey through the heartbreak can feel like a free fall, causing every impulse in us to fight against having our bodies slammed into the ground. With our instincts calibrated toward self-preservation and the ground quickly rushing up to meet us, making a choice to be broken open instead of broken apart seems futile at worst and a luxury at best. The goal, it often seems, is simply to get out alive—no matter who gets trampled in the process.

But there is hope. There is, indeed, a beautiful alternative. This is not the way it's meant to be. We don't need to settle for life with our defenses up. We can lower our guard and use that energy for something else. We can get our focus back.

EIGHT

BEYOND OUR WILDEST IMAGINATION

I admit I go through life with my nose to the grindstone, my shoulder to the wheel. I don't always think of Jesus when I open my eyes in the morning. Instead, I'm usually more preoccupied with how much more sleep I can sneak in before swinging my legs over the edge of the bed to deal with the dishes in the sink from the night before, the current state of my bank account, or the pain in my right shoulder and what that pain might suggest about my mortality. I fully relate to all the ways we struggle to infuse our faith into the everydayness of life.

But I do often try to imagine what might happen if we could find our way back to childlike wonder. Do you remember wonder?

Looking for New

When Dutch visionary Theo Jansen took his Strandbeests to New England, the children in the crowds were enthralled by the lifelike movements of these creatures—giant lifelike structures Jansen crafts using PVC pipes connected together with plastic ties and powered by the wind. When I first watched on TV these spectacular creatures moving their way down the beach, I was bug-eyed with awe. It was as if I'd come face-to-face with the future—and with something I never could have imagined in my wildest dreams. I felt a mixture of fear and fascination. I kept stopping the footage, rewinding, and playing it again.

"What is it that brings out the child in us when we see these objects?" CBS news anchor, Jamie Wax asked when he interviewed Jansen about the effect his Strandbeests had on the crowd. Jansen replied, "For a child, life is new, right? Every experience is new and, if you see something new, you forget you've grown up, and the child comes back."[1]

When was the last time you saw something new? When was the last time you tried something new? When was the last time you went somewhere new? When was the last time you met someone new? When was the last time you dreamed up something new?

Newness originates with God. "I am making all things new," he tells us in Revelation 21:5. Do you live expectantly? Are you on the lookout for *new*? Because God is consistently promising us *new*, we have to be intentional about releasing what we've always known and how we've always done things in order to get a glimpse of where God is excitedly inviting us to venture. "Be like children," Jesus says to us (see Matt. 18:3), and it sounds as if he's saying, "Stand up on your tiptoes! Expect the unexpected! Live as if it's always Christmas Eve!"

"Forget the former things," God urges us (Isa. 43:18). "I'm doing something brand new, here and now! Don't you see it? It's right there, in front of you!"

Children don't have a corner on the wonder market, although I suspect we would agree that they are better at using their imaginations and living in awe and with wonder. Still, they do not have a monopoly on imagination. And we can learn from their example. They do not let their imaginations become stunted by inhibitions. They don't have enough history to fall back into old habits. Everything is new to children. Each day arrives on their pillow with a healthy dose of expectancy. They let their imaginations run wild, and we, the adults in the room, are giddy in our encouragement of them. To a point. Sadly, somewhere on the journey, someone teaches the child to put her imagination in check. "Inappropriate," the adult in the room declares. "Impolite," the stick-in-the-mud whispers. "Illogical," says the imagine-less bossypants. "Impossible," says whoever. And the nail is hammered into the coffin.

Thank God for resurrection.

Our hair color, our height, our skin tone, and our eye color are gifts to us from God. So is our imagination. Just as we, in spirit, mind, and body, reflect the image of God in this world, we also reflect his image through our imaginations. We are, each of us, *imago Dei*, which mean "image of God." Even our imagination is *imago Dei*. The word *imagination* springs forth from that Latin word *imago*, from the verb *imaginari*, which is to say, "picture to oneself."

Our understanding of *imago Dei* takes on even more richness when we grasp that we are not only created with God's image imprinted on us, but *we also reflect God's image back to God.*

Our imaginations allow us to create a picture for ourselves (in our minds, as we have come to understand it) of a thing that does not (yet) exist or that is not in our tangible presence. Something brand new! The image of God in us prods us to reach for and believe that what we have been promised will come to pass, even though we cannot see it. This is the very definition of faith—taking God at his word and acting as if it is so, even though we can't see it. Yet.

God is always pointing us forward, into what we do not yet see and cannot even imagine. But we can try.

God is the author of all new ideas, images, and concepts of objects that we cannot see with our limited, mortal senses. Even when we stretch our imaginations to their furthest reaches, we have not stretched far enough. The Bible tells us that what God has in store for us has not even entered into our consciousness. So let's reach forward for those things that lie ahead, as those who carry the very Spirit of the living God in our beings. As children of God, our sanctified imaginations are the catalyst for dreaming bigger dreams, and these include dreams of oneness and unity, just as Jesus prayed for us.

Planting New Paradigms

Long before I was born, my paternal grandfather was an agricultural extension agent in rural Virginia. In his role, my grandfather traveled around from farm to farm, teaching landowners in his African American community to *cultivate* the soil in a manner that produced the greatest yield of crops. Through his work, my grandfather helped farmers develop the best environment for their crops to flourish. I can't think of a better word picture for who we are as culture makers in the world.

Culture making is a sacred reflection of the God-in-us. It is our response to God's call to humanity to cultivate the world we've been given. Just as *imago Dei* and *imagination* share an etymology, so do the words *culture* and *cultivate*.

Our efforts in policy, technology, the arts, religion, medicine, and athletics are (theoretically) focused on creating an environment that facilitates the vibrant physical, intellectual, and spiritual growth of its inhabitants. Culture is the manifestation of these efforts. It is defined as "the beliefs, customs, arts, etc., of a particular society, group, place, or time."[2] Culture is what we are making in our day-to-day interactions and through the work of our hands.

Our prayers.

Our conversations at the dinner table.

Our actions in the public square.

Our kneading of dough.

Our correspondences.

Our tending of the garden.

Our dance moves.

Our worship.

Our poetry.

Our brushstrokes on canvas.

Our architecture.

Our bedside watches through the night.

Our sermons.

Our music.

Our scientific studies.

Our measuring and cutting.

Our response to our enemies.

All of these and more, when surrendered to God the Creator, play a role in cultivating an environment in which oneness and unity can flourish.

God is making all things new, and he has invited us to be his hands and feet in the world.

God invites us to be kingdom-come people. On earth, as it is in heaven. Tilling the ground. Cultivating the places he leads us so that oneness and unity can thrive. Planting new paradigms, right in the middle of the way we've always done things. This way of living is countercultural, and it doesn't look like anything we're used to.

It might feel as if pursuing anything other than the life we're used to will result in chaos. But what if that's not so bad.

My husband often tells the story of watching a crew of contractors building our neighbor's new carport over the course of days and weeks. To build the new carport, the old one had to be torn down. Using a backhoe and other construction equipment, the contractors demolished the old carport in just a matter of hours. What remained was a complete mess in our neighbor's driveway and my astonished husband watching from across the field. The carport that had stood in that spot just a few hours before had seemed completely functional from my husband's perspective. Now, looking at the heap of mangled metal and splintered wood, my husband thought our neighbor had made a huge mistake. But, over the next day or so, the contractors removed the pile of rubble that had once stood as a carport. Then, slowly and deliberately, the contractors constructed a brand-new carport, which, even to my untrained eyes, was exceedingly better than the one that had stood in its place just a short time before.

Here's the thing about that story. Those of us who find ourselves in the midst of chaos often mistake the chaos as failure. We see ourselves as having taken the proverbial two steps back before taking any steps forward. It's important to remember, however, that God is always moving us toward the preferred future he has prepared for us. With this in mind, even what looks like chaos may be progress. In the case of our neighbor's carport, the new construction never could have been built without first destroying the old one. So, while the result of demolition was a chaotic pile of rubble, that pile of rubble was a step in the right direction. It was a step toward something brand new.

In fact, God first looked out at chaos and spoke into it, bringing an entirely new world into existence. As his children, created in his image and instilled with the power of the Holy Spirit, we are invited to bring our sanctified imagination to each experience, even the ones that seem to be the most chaotic. Riots. Terrorism. Racism. Sexism. Abuse. Trafficking. Betrayal. Brutality. Illness. Death. Grief. Bring your sanctified imagination to the tables, my brothers and sisters.

God's words to us speak of sons and daughters prophesying, old men dreaming dreams, and young men seeing visions. What a delightful and mystifying promise. This is who we are. We are the prophets, the dreamers, the visionaries.

Jesus knew the world and its people would find oneness to be an impossible dream. He knew we would have a hard time getting beyond the limitations of the physical world. Beyond walls. Beyond bodies. Beyond language, and more. Christ's appeal to God for our oneness and unity—with God, with ourselves, and with others—is the same creative agency that inspired God in the beginning to say, "Let there be . . . "

Our Heritage, Our Legacy

Not long ago, a man was beheaded on international television. It was horrifying to watch. Even now, I have to pause and take a deep breath at the thought of it. One man, under the influence of evil, carried out a terrible act against another man. To say it was tragic is nowhere near the right term for the event. After the incident, I could feel fear creeping around the edges of my heart, eager for an opportunity to soak into my thoughts and influence my actions. I watched as people in my community began to give in to the fear, putting their sanctified imaginations on lockdown and shrinking in the face of the chaos that began to emerge. Newscasters began to call the man by a name that his mother had not given him, a name that was nothing but a characterization of the horrifying action he had taken.

I heard the nickname come across the airwaves and immediately recognized it for what it was: a lack of imagination and a door swung wide for evil to enter in. For me, calling this man by that nickname would have been setting a brick in a wall that fear wanted built between this man and me. Each time I used the name, I'd be setting another brick in the wall. Despair would grow and settle around each brick like mortar, setting in the blaze of a flame that looked a lot like hate. So I refused to use the name. Even now, I will not say it. Dehumanizing a person by taking away their name is one of the surest paths to division, discrimination, marginalization, and hatred. If you've ever been on the receiving end of a round of name-calling, you know what I'm talking about. And if you've ever been the one doing the name-calling (sadly, I have), you know where that comes from and where it leads.

In the wake of the televised beheading, I could sense a gentle question forming in my soul. I can only attribute this to the kind leadership of the Holy Spirit. I was just as shaken as everyone else who knew of the beheading. I was just as susceptible to the influence of evil that wanted me to fear and then hate this man and everyone who reminded me of him. I knew I could justify my anger as righteousness and rationalize any revenge as reasonable. But the Holy Spirit continued to gently lead me to the question that rose to the surface of my soul: "What name did his mother give him?"

To God, it was not enough for me to refuse to use the man's nickname. God wanted me to know his given name. God wanted me to think of this man's mother, just as I had thought about and prayed and grieved for the mother of the son who had perished. God wanted me to identify with this man's mother, so that I could identify with her son.

I found his name (it only took a quick search on my computer), wrote it on a small square of paper, and taped that paper to the window above my kitchen sink. Whenever I saw the name, I could see him only the way I think God must have seen him: beloved. And so I prayed for him. I prayed for his safety. For his salvation. For his peace. The more I prayed for him, the less I feared him. When I learned he had been killed, I felt a sadness in my heart, not unlike the sadness I had felt for the man he'd beheaded. This is the transformative power of God to reconcile us to one another, even when it seems impossible.

So from now on we regard no one from a worldly point of view. Though we once regarded Christ in this way, we do so no longer. Therefore, if anyone is in Christ, the new creation has come: The old has gone, the new is here! All this is from God, who reconciled us to himself through Christ and gave us the ministry of reconciliation: that God was reconciling the world to himself in Christ, not counting people's sins against them. And he has committed to us the message of reconciliation. We are therefore Christ's ambassadors, as though God were making his appeal through us. (2 Cor. 5:16–20)

When terrorists terrorize, abusers abuse, traffickers traffic, and oppressors oppress, they cultivate an environment in which chaos thrives. This is nothing new. Their behavior has been birthed in chaos, and it begets chaos. This kind of chaos is the way of this world. We should not be stunned. Nor should we be deterred. This kind of chaos also leaves a void. As Christians, we can step away and allow evil to fill the void, or we can step up, speak out, and cultivate an environment in which all things come together under God's mighty hand.

Believe it or not, God desires that even terrorists, abusers, and oppressors be reconciled to him, to themselves, and to one another. And yes, God has given us the Holy Spirit and made us agents—like my grandfather, all those years ago—creating and teaching others to foster an environment in which oneness and unity flourish. We are agents of reconciliation. This is our heritage, our legacy. The ministry of bringing our sanctified imagination into a world of chaos is our divine privilege. When we see the world burst apart under the stress of terror and fear, oppression and despair, we are the ones who know this is not all there is. We reach forward, expecting that God is doing something new, even when we find it impossible to believe. We reach as far as we can, and then the Spirit of God extends our reach and transforms our perspective so that it is one with his.

Let's surrender our imaginations to the will and the wonder of the Spirit. This wonder grounds itself in things that are bigger than us and beyond our wildest imagination. It moves us to the edges of our collective seats in anticipation of something we have never seen or even dreamed. This kind of wonder is the spark of creative anticipation that awakens our spirits to the spectacular truth that God, indeed, is making all things new.

NINE

ONE WITH OURSELVES

A few years ago, I found myself to be part of what had been unceremoniously dubbed the "sandwich generation." We were characterized by being in a stage of life in which our duties had us ping-ponging back and forth between caring for aging parents and young children. We spent daytime hours shuttling parents to different doctor appointments and consultations. Our evenings were spent on the sidelines of our child's soccer games or seated at a tiny desk for parent-teacher conferences. I was a prime example.

Although my mother-in-law lived far away, her health challenges were front and center for my husband and me. Daily phone calls with doctors and health care facilities kept us on edge and concerned. At the same time, our children were both in high school, and although they could drive themselves to school and other events, we still wanted to support them in their hobbies and activities.

One morning I stood in the shower, exhausted before the day had even begun. I let the water run over me in the hopes that it would wake me up. Taking a mental inventory of all the things on that day's to-do list, I began to feel stretched thin, like a bubble-gum bubble about to pop. I covered my face with both hands and shouted into my palms, "I'm a piece of bologna!" I felt the full weight of my position in the sandwich generation fall squarely on my shoulders.

Eventually, I realized the error of my ways. I was a wife, a mother, a daughter-in-law, an employee, a writer, and more. What I didn't realize was that I had been compartmentalizing myself according to each of those titles or roles in my life. As a result, instead of being fully engaged in each event—talking with my husband about his mother's health, cheering for my daughter at a basketball game, cooking dinner in my kitchen—I was only bringing a part of me to each experience.

Over time, I learned instead to give my full attention to each event or situation and, contrary to what you might think, I had more energy, more focus, and less stress as a result.

Many of us are living fragmented lives. We divide ourselves up, trying to be all things to all people, all at the same time. But that is God's role, not ours. Our role is to bring our full selves to every encounter, every conversation, every experience. What we can do, better than anyone else, is to be our fullest selves in every moment and with every person we meet. No fragmentation. No division.

All Is Sacred

One way we often divide ourselves is by categorizing our work and activities as either sacred or secular. Even this, God invites us to reconsider.

Something that is secular is said to have no religious or spiritual basis. When I step back and let that meaning sink in, I am hard-pressed to find much of anything in this world that I might consider secular. Oh, yes, there are systems, programs, attitudes, and ideas that have, indeed, become corrupt and tragically and horrifically compromised by the influence of evil in the world. But we often stop short of exercising the great influence we bear as God's ambassadors of reconciliation when we throw our hands in the air and proclaim that she or it or they are beyond the reach of God's great power and desire to restore. When that happens, we should probably take a breath and check to see where we might have left our imagination.

As followers of Jesus and members of the body of Christ, everything about us has been made new. This, of course, is a mystery. We hear and read the words telling us we are new—the old has gone, and the new has come.[1] "New creations!" we hear the preacher tell us. We listen and nod in agreement as we try to reconcile the truth of those words with what we still know to be true about ourselves. We know we are sinners and that, when pushed just far enough or left alone long enough, we still have that old way of being dominating some parts of our lives. Old preachers used to call it the old nature, the sin nature, the old man, the sinful man. Sometimes it seemed this old man (or woman) would get the best of us and cause us to fall back into relying on old habits and making foolish mistakes.

Paul talks about this too. On and on he laments about how hard it is to live a sinless life. "Who will rescue me from this body that is subject to death?" he asks.[2] I read those words and picture a scraggly version of Paul, sitting at the end of a bar, a few sheets to the wind, his five-o'clock-shadowed chin in one hand and a tumbler of bourbon in his hand. Neat.

We've been there ourselves, and if you haven't yet, just keep on living. We've been right in the spot where we try to reconcile our sinful nature with the promise we've been given that we are new creatures and are free, indeed.

Knowing what we know about ourselves, it's easy to want to explain it by dividing the world into sacred and secular. In this kind of dualistic world, it's easier to categorize and label our actions as one or the other. This or that. Good or bad. Right or wrong. Holy or not holy.

As this kind of dualistic reckoning weaves itself through my view of the world, I begin to think of my life, work, and extracurricular activities as one or the other too. My Sunday morning church attendance is sacred, and my Monday through Friday work life is secular. My night at the club is secular, but the messiness of that gets washed away when I spend a sacred hour doing penance or ten good deeds. Monday through Friday at the dinner table with family might be sacred, unless someone starts talking about politics or unpaid bills or the neighbor who keeps blasting that loud music when the baby is sleeping. On Saturday, I run secular errands and then gather with my sacred small group. In each instance, I find myself checking my posture, my language, my behavior, and my outfit to make sure it fits the correct sacred or secular theme and gives off the correct vibe. And let's keep it real: I check yours too.

All this shifting from sacred to secular has me straddling a massive fault line that runs through the center of my soul. I end up fragmented, and I marginalize parts of myself from the life-giving work of the Holy Spirit. When I label parts of my life as secular, I will eventually come to believe these secular parts of me aren't worthy of taking into God's presence. My twisted thinking leaves me hoarding and hiding parts of my life and myself from the restorative work of Christ. So I limp along, hindering myself by trying to straddle an imaginary divide in my soul that doesn't exist. Paul, not one to mince words, writes about this as being double-minded: "Such a person is double-minded and unstable in all they do" (James 1:8).

Oneness within Us

In the prayer captured in John 17, Jesus was praying not only for oneness *among* his followers but also for oneness *within* each follower. We cannot be at one with others if we aren't at one with ourselves. This oneness plays itself out and comes to life inside of us in what we've come to know as integrity.

How do you know if this double-mindedness is at work in your own soul? Here are some indicators to consider: when you lack integrity in your relationships, it shows up as secrecy, unfaithfulness, and shallowness (which looks like a constant focus on yourself rather than on the other person or people involved). Lack of integrity in business or work shows up as a poor work ethic, lack of focus, and consistent failure to follow through on commitments. Lack of integrity in leadership shows up as lack of respect, lack of trust, and lack of a strong and consistent moral code.[3]

One thing I find most attractive about a person is when they are consistently the same person, no matter where I encounter them. Their integrity reflects a love of self that isn't flashy or brash or egotistical. Integrity is hard won and worth fighting for. People with integrity are not conflicted within themselves about who they believe someone else wants them to be. They know themselves and have made peace with whatever that means. Additionally, when a person of integrity has a relationship with Christ, they can embrace the person God created them to be with great enthusiasm and as worship back to God. In fact, the gift of integrity is often the by-product of growing oneness with God, through his Son, Jesus, and empowered by the Holy Spirit.

People with this kind of spiritual integrity read the words in Genesis about God looking out over everything he made and proclaiming that it was good, and they believe them. They understand (without having to determine whether it was over the course of seven days or seven millennia) that they were created in the very image of God—not as God and not equal to God, but as a part of God's creation that carries the glory of God through the world. They believe that when God made humanity as spirit, mind, *and* body, he looked at what he had made and said, "Now *that* is very good!"

It is hard work to live with a deep fault line down the center of your soul, believing part of you (often your soul) is good and part of you (often your body) is not. By dividing ourselves into good and bad, we have no choice but to feel shame for parts of ourselves or, at the very least, to value parts of ourselves less.

Our societies have set themselves up to reinforce these hierarchies that we establish against ourselves. American culture, especially, favors extroverts and people who can read. We value those who can speak and understand English and people who recycle. We don't (publicly) have much tolerance for people who are addicted to substances or get caught cheating on their spouse or riot or tell racist, sexist, or homophobic jokes. Our antipathy grows deeper when these people refuse to apologize or "get help" or pay back their "debt to society."

We give names to these people, which is a big mistake. Because when we label someone a junkie or a thug or a racist or a homewrecker or a gold digger or a terrorist, we have taken a side against the image of God in them. We have set grace to the side. We have stepped in the pathway between them and the power of God to redeem, restore, and reconcile that person to himself.

When I am living with a fault line in my own soul, unfortunately I also *need* the world to be divided along a fault line of sacred and secular in order to live with myself. I need someone against whom I can compare my own brokenness and say, "Well, at least I'm not as bad as . . ."

Oneness in Others

All of these divides depend on the notion that a person or a group of people is less sacred than another. But the truth we've been given is that all life is sacred. If all life is sacred, then *all* life is sacred in spirit, mind, and body. Every now and then, our culture needs to be reminded of certain members of our population and their value in the eyes of God. This is evidenced through the work of those who advocate on behalf of unborn children, homeless veterans, the mentally ill, victims of sexual assault, and many more.

Movements like Black Lives Matter raise awareness of the value of those who, in the words of Michelle Alexander, "we as a nation have learned not to care about."[4] These movements don't exalt one group above any others. These movements remind us of the *imago Dei* in each person we meet.

As Christians, we are quick to accept that a person's spirit is sacred. We are invested, often too much, in the salvation and redemption of the spirit of a person at the expense of the body. But it is incumbent on us to view each person in full, and when we do, we become more invested in saving one another's body too. If my soul deserves to be protected and saved, then so does my body, no matter how I've treated it, what language it understands, or what sins it may have committed.

When we fail to recognize each person's wholeness and can no longer see the sacredness in their mind and body (particularly when they think or do something we don't agree with, cannot support, or don't understand), we are walking on shaky ground. Just as it is dangerous when we minimize any aspect of ourselves, it is dangerous to minimize any aspect of any other person we encounter. They too have been created by God and are dearly loved by God. Their gender, skin color, hair color and texture, body type, and freckles are God's handiwork. Their perspective on the world is the result of the sum of their life experiences at the moment you and I first encounter them. Wishing away or seeking to silence some aspect of another person is the same as sending them to the other side of some imaginary fault line, where their gender or skin color or worldview is irredeemable at worst, and insignificant at best.

Yes, some behaviors, actions, and systems perpetuate evil in this world. They reflect the great imaginary fault lines around which entire societies stagger, trying not to fall in and blaming one another for the great divides. We can feed this insanity, or we can refuse to let it triumph over us. What that looks like will be different for every single one of us, but our response to evil is rooted in what we know to be true about our standing in the eyes of God.

Ordinary Heroes

We often compare our understanding of where we stand with God to what we read about others and how they have responded under some of the most horrific circumstances. We read books and go to lectures and listen to experts who tell us about missionaries and martyrs and ministry giants who seem transfigured into bona fide superheroes. I am certainly not trying to minimize their courage, bravery, and faith. But when we try to imagine ourselves in their shoes and wonder how we would have behaved, we often imagine ourselves falling short of their supernatural example. The truth, however, is that their story is theirs and ours is ours. Whatever you and I may face in our regular, ordinary days is where we live out our courage, bravery, and faith.

When I read these stories, I am struck by the integrity of these heroes amid great hardship and even death. I wonder if I too have a soul free from a fault line that divides me against myself. I wonder if I've been keeping parts of myself hidden from God's great love and mercy. I wonder if that fault line in my soul will be able to support me when the pressure bears down. I know the answer to that question, even if I never articulate it. You too?

Perhaps this is why we are so easily swayed by fear.

Jesus knew our divided souls would leave us wide open, sitting ducks, really, to the strategies that have their foundations in the brokering of fear. That's why the Bible repeatedly tells us not to fear. It even makes clear that fear does not come from

God. "God," the Bible says, "has not given us a spirit of fear" (2 Tim. 1:7 NKJV). If you are watching the news and begin to feel fearful, know God is not communicating that feeling through the screen. Fear multiplies itself quickly if we are not careful. We want to get on the other side of fear, seeking to identify who's responsible for it. We yearn to distance ourselves from it—and from its source.

Fear's purpose is to warn us of potential danger so that we can take the appropriate steps to protect ourselves and those we love. Fear works to separate me from something that (or someone who) poses a direct threat to me. I see or sense danger and, in the interest of self-preservation, I go in a different direction. Often, when I am incited to fear another person, it is because I've been led to believe that person poses a threat to me.

Here is where it's important to pay attention. This is where it matters that we come to understand the value of the spirit, mind, and body together as one. When I am able to recognize that no lines divide my life or myself into categories of either sacred or secular, more or less valuable, I can understand that about you too. Integrity calls me to be *for* you, and not against you. Integrity calls for me to see you from a sacred perspective. God never looks at you, or at anyone, and considers you worthless. What makes me think I am the judge of who is worthless or beyond God's ability to redeem? I may not agree with your perspective, but I can be for you. We can be for one another. Imagine the message such support for one another could send to the rest of the world.

The things that we are for give us access to places and people that others don't have. Being for one thing does not give us a license to bash someone who is for something else—even if that something else is opposite of what I am for.

162

Laying Down My Life

I have to be just as willing to lay down my life for the terrorist, the sex offender, the drug trafficker, and the rogue politician as I am for the terrorized, the trafficked, the marginalized, and the disenfranchised. Truly and honestly, as I read the Scriptures, I don't see any other way. If I am so invested in my position or my country or my comfort or my life that I cannot love a stranger or my enemy, then those things have become idols. It is hard to live without these idols in our repertoire. For so many of us, life is good and the temptation is strong to keep it that way.

What kind of world would this be if, knowing that our lives would make way for someone else to get to God, we quit hanging on so tightly to our lives? I mean, what are we hanging on to? We've already got all of the promises of Jesus and eternity with God. So can I hold my life loosely enough to be willing to sacrifice it in case it is one day required of me, to make space for someone else to have time to make her way to Jesus?

What is the purpose of my life? What is the value of it and for what—or for whom—would I offer it up?

Many of us feel in our hearts—without giving it a second thought—that we would die for a loved one. For a child, a parent, a dear friend, or a spouse. But Jesus asks us to first bless those who curse us, pray for those who mistreat us.[5] Jesus is well aware that speaking a blessing over someone, or praying for them, changes the person doing the blessing and the praying. We might look for change in the person who is the object of the blessing or the prayer, but it may never be evident to us. We are faced squarely with the prospect of checking our motivation when we are blessing or praying for a person we'd really rather cuss out. If our motivation is merely to heap burning coals on the head of our offender, well, that's a great starting point in the sense that we have started and are not standing still. But that is not the point, is it? I think Jesus knew what he was up to, don't you? Maybe we know that in our hearts too—not only our heads. It can be incredibly difficult to move in the direction of being *for* the people the world has told us are our enemies. But remember: members of the body of Christ have only one true enemy, and it is not one another.

For You

There is nothing new under the sun. Throughout history, we have been choosing sides against one another, and our passions have been manipulated and twisted by the enemy. He keeps us fighting against one another—endlessly debating "the issue." We get tricked by those who say we should choose a side. It seems, however, that Scripture instructs us to choose to be *for* people. All people. Period. No exceptions.

Consider all the things that could change if we were truly *for* people. What would it look like for us to embrace and celebrate the *imago Dei* in each person? What could that change in our world? How would that create kingdom come?

Of course, there is tension between caring for the people for whom we are responsible and being *for* all others too. It is a narrow road to traverse. It's difficult to know where to set your foot next, isn't it? We do our best. We pray. We pray some more. Either way, we live with the consequences of our choices. This is the fallout and wreckage of the influence of evil on humanity. Because we are *in* the world, we are sometimes in the unfortunate position of finding ourselves in the devastating path (literally and figuratively) of a bullet—either a stray one or one aimed directly at us or someone we love. This is not conjecture. We try to protect ourselves, but we cannot fool ourselves into thinking we will escape pain, grief, suffering, or torment in this world. We are living in a fallen kingdom. We are bound to catch cold here from time to time.

So the question isn't whether we will suffer. Instead, the question is, how will we respond when suffering comes our way? How will we respond if our life is required of us?

Is this not at the heart of our wide divides? If your opinion, lifestyle, or quest for power appears as if they might threaten my life—and by that, I mean my actual life, as well as my comfort or safety or position or power—my gut reaction is to cut you off and cut you out. But this flies in the face of Christ's sacrifice and death on the cross. Jesus died with open arms, inviting all who would, to come to him and be healed. For this life—and for eternity.

The only time Jesus really got mad was at church people (see John 2:13–17). People who were making it difficult to get to God. That day in the temple, he may have thrown people out, but Jesus didn't cut them off or cut them out. He does not turn against us. We are the ones who turn.

When I strive to keep my comfort, power, or convenience intact, I am working for something that will eventually fade away. But when my goal is love, blessing, and prayer, my work is established in the kingdom of God. We cannot love both. Not really. We cannot love God and something or someone else equally. Loving God first makes it possible for us to love our enemies. That is the command—to love the people we would claim as our enemies.

The *imago Dei* is in each of us, and we study God so that we know him when we see him. So we can spot him. Or, if we can't see him—if he's gotten lost or clouded over to the point that we can't pick him out—we still bless. We still pray. Because it matters. And, if nothing else, it changes us.

TEN

RETURN TO HOME

We are human. Mortal. Finite. We are not invincible. We break. We hurt. We fall. Neither the work of reconciliation nor the vision of oneness comes without cost. Recognizing when the costs have depleted your reserves is not a sign of weakness. On the contrary. Realizing it's time to take a break, and then taking one, is a sign of both wisdom and strength.

There are support groups, movements, ministries, and businesses established solely for the advancement of the notion of self-care. At the end of *Another Round*, a popular podcast, hosts Heben and Tracy encourage listeners to take their meds, call their moms, drink more water, and back up their data. These are aspects of self-care, and the reminders from the podcast hosts serve as an acknowledgment of our need to slow down and breathe deeply from time to time. We have limitations.

If you care for others—whether through the work of reconciliation, advocacy, protest, community organizing, ministry, or parenting—you would be wise to practice self-care with intentionality and persistence. There are many ways to practice self-care, including taking the steps necessary to be kind and stay healthy, like Heben and Tracy remind their listeners to do. But many forms of self-care can be categorized as either furlough or sabbatical.

Furlough

Missionaries and deployed combat troops are acquainted with the concept of furlough. During a furlough, an individual leaves the place where they are serving and returns to the people and places they call home. In other words, a furlough is when we leave the unfamiliar for a time in order to reconnect with what is most familiar to us.

When we first moved to Nebraska, everything about our new community was unfamiliar to us. The customs and conversations were difficult for us to grasp. Even the topography was unsettling and disorienting. I felt rattled at a deep level for a very long time. Even now, after having lived in Nebraska for more than a decade, I sometimes find myself jolted, yet again, by the realization that this place is not innate to me. The nature of Nebraska, no matter how fluent I become in it, will always be my second language. My story has Nebraska in it, but Nebraska is not where I grew my roots.

This return to our roots is the essence of furlough. My parents no longer live in the state where I grew up, yet when I visit them in their home, I am closest to my roots—to the things that grounded me and set my foundation. You know this feeling too if you have ever come back home after spending time in a place that required you to constantly be alert to different customs, language patterns, food, scents, and values. When we return home, we are able to let down our guard. As a result, our minds and bodies are more fully able to process the lessons we've learned from our experiences in unfamiliar places. Likewise, a furlough is designed to protect our mental health. We gain space so that we can begin to process the ways the people and experiences in our places of service are impacting and influencing us. Because they are. From our home base, we can allow God to transform us as he synthesizes our experiences. The process renews our minds, and as the Bible tells us, this renewal of our minds is the foundation of transformation. So when we return to our location of service, we do so with a clearer understanding of how our gifts and passions meet the needs of the places we are called to serve.

In addition to transforming our minds, being on furlough also expands our minds. When we are ensconced in the daily grind of service in less familiar places, it is often difficult to see the impact of our work or the small glimpses of growth along the way. We succumb to drudgery and routine. Without furlough, our experience presses in on us, making it difficult to see the forest for the trees. If you are feeling burned out, irritated, or irrelevant; if you've lost your vision and the passion for your calling, consider returning home.

Home, of course, may not be the place where you grew up. It may not be among people who share your DNA. Home is where people know your story and don't hold it against you. It is where you feel the least guarded. For me, home is loud, with people talking over one another and food cooking on the stove and bare feet and laughing until my sides ache. It is the unconditional love of my parents and shopping at the dollar stores with my mom. It is sitting on the porch swing in the summertime, watching my dad mow the lawn.

Where is home for you? Who are the people who know you best? One way to identify home is to think about the very first people with whom you would share the best news about yourself. That is the place to go, and those are the people to surround yourself with—intentionally and at regular intervals. When a real home is unavailable due to distance, timing, loss, or expense, a proxy works well too.

Recently, I was feeling the weight of this emptiness that comes from serving in unfamiliar places. It had been a long time since I'd been to any version of home. I should pause here and say that the home I have in Nebraska with my husband is wonderful. It is full of love, laughter, harmony, and music. We have an easy way about us, and we weave his structured personality together with my spontaneous flitting about. We have a thing and our groove is serious and well-oiled. But we are both far from the places where we grew our roots. We are both far from the culture that gave us our first language, and sometimes we both need a dose of that kind of home.

When my recent longing for home arrived—for Motown, "Please pass the sweet tea," and my cousin showing up for dinner just in time—it could not have been better timed. That very week, a cable channel aired an awards show called *Black Girls Rock*. It was an elegantly extravagant celebration of strong black women. For three hours, I sat on my couch and watched as beautiful black and brown women of all ages, abilities, sizes, and shapes filled my television screen with their talent and wisdom, style and grace.

My night of watching "Black Girls Rock" was not elevating my culture above the culture in which I serve, it was a feast for my hungry soul. It grounded me and helped reconcile me, once again, to myself. I was reminded of the history and values

I bring with me from home and share in the places I serve. I was reminded that these things are good and solid and full of merit. I was also able to see how the place where I serve and the people with whom I labor have taught me, refined me, and anchored me. Amid a culture in which I often find it difficult to obtain such specific affirmation, I was able to celebrate who God made me to be. Watching "Black Girls Rock" and crying through each acceptance speech made me better equipped to reenlist in the work of reconciliation from a posture of grace and love. Culture can minister to us in this way. Culture can restore us to the body, even better than we were before.

I recorded the show, and I will watch it again and again—in those moments when my heart longs for the place where my roots took hold. The recorded program is a proxy for home. It will serve as a mini-furlough when I can't get home to the strong black women in my family and the incredible men who support us.

Missionaries and military personnel have seasons of furlough scheduled into their service programs. Depending on the type of work they do, these individuals may be required to return home at regular intervals. Those of us doing the work of reconciliation with a goal of oneness often operate in unfamiliar cultures and surroundings and among people who see the world differently from us. Consequently, furloughs are imperative. We won't all be able to negotiate furloughs into our work contracts, but it is certainly worth a try for those who can see a way to make it happen. Leaders of organizations and entrepreneurs who focus on reconciliation should consider how to ensure that workers at every level have an opportunity to experience some type of furlough at intervals that work well for everyone.

Time away for furlough protects our mental, physical, and spiritual well-being. It is time spent with people and in places that are most familiar to us. Furlough grounds us, once again, in our foundational beliefs and reconnects us with the significant cultural touchpoints that frame our life story.

Sabbath

A sabbatical is different from a furlough in that it helps to give us wings. Sharing an etymology with the word *Sabbath*, a sabbatical is also about stepping out of the rat race in order to recalibrate our perspective. While we don't necessarily have to go anywhere to experience a sabbatical, we do want to be sure our sabbatical takes place in an environment that shifts our focus. A sabbatical should always involve a fast, or a break, from the ordinary trappings of our regular lives. If the internet is part of your daily life (as is the case for me), then a sabbatical might include a fast from the web. If most of your day is spent indoors, take an outdoor sabbatical. If you are usually the one caring for others, paying for a professional massage for yourself counts as sabbatical. If noise makes up a good part of your ordinary days (whether by design or not), try a sabbatical of silence. If yours is a life of leaving, take a sabbatical of staying put.

If you are fortunate to actually be able to get away for a vacation (and Americans, especially, need to stop treating "vacation" as if it's a dirty word), then go! No glory exists in carrying over all of your vacation days into future years. It's not a savings account. Vacation days do not accrue interest. Use them. Go camping or hiking. Fly to an exotic beach and only pack bikinis and bottles of sunscreen. Head to the mountains and ski in powder. Spend a week at a monastery or get your yoga certification. Learn how to make flan. Find the best restaurant for eating flan. Sit in your backyard and read an entire book. Some people can take their vacation time and go on a short-term mission trip, and that works for them. It fills them up. If that's you, great! That is not me. If it's not you either, don't sweat it. Go on a mission trip if you feel led to do so. But if you still need a vacation after your mission trip, take one! Please.

My friend Sam regularly leads groups of students on extreme (to me) outdoor adventures. Just today I received a message from Sam. He is headed to Peru tomorrow for twenty-one days, along with thirteen college students and two coleaders. These trips are a joy for Sam, and he pours everything he has into the experience. Over the years, however, Sam learned the important distinction between a change of scenery and a true sabbatical. In fact, some sabbaticals take place at home, in the form of a staycation. The point, remember, is to shift your focus, even if you can't change your surroundings.

A sabbatical should also serve to restore your spirit, mind, and body. To this end, my friend Sam taught me to buffer my speaking engagements with "me time." Now, when my ministry requires that I travel to speak to a group or at a conference in a different town or state, I plan an extra day or two after the trip as vacation. These extra days are a brief sabbatical—or Sabbath. When I book the speaking event on my calendar, I include the extra days as part of the event. Even if all I plan to do is sit on my couch in my living room and stare out my window. This recovery time is important because, even though I had a change of scenery while I was away, the opportunity to serve as a speaker at an event means I give my whole self to the experience. It is definitely a joy and an honor and probably my favorite part of ministry. However, the restorative time of sabbatical happens for me after the event is over, the venue has cleared out, and the participants have had their own spirits restored.

One point I want to stress to others who may travel for ministry as I do: your travel days are not sabbatical days. Travel days are unpredictable and often add stress to our lives. Many times, I've found myself ministering on the plane to a seatmate. While the Holy Spirit always gives me the extra amount of alertness and presence required during these high-altitude opportunities, they often drain me even more. Sometimes travel days are peaceful and uncomplicated. When this happens, be grateful, thank God, and still plan to take a day off when you get back home.

Reconciled for Reconciling

I often wonder what Jesus's days would have looked like if they were mapped out on a calendar. He didn't seem to be constrained by time or schedules. Jesus, the ultimate reconciler, gave himself fully to every encounter. We know the work he did while he lived among humanity drained him. The Bible even tells us Jesus felt the power go out of him as he moved among us (see Luke 8:46). Jesus understood the costs involved with loving, serving, and building bridges to oneness. He knew more than we ever will the toll of restoring individuals, organizations, and nations to wholeness. Yet, as he reminded us so clearly, even he didn't have a place to lay his head. And for those of us who might become weary of serving the people God has given to us, take heart. Even Jesus cried out, in frustration, "How much longer do I have to be with you?"

This work God invites us to share with him has a cost. Knowing the cost, Jesus made a point to steal away for private times of restoration. In those moments, Jesus modeled for us the importance of the continuing work of reconciliation with God and with ourselves. He knew that time away from our work and our surroundings serves to reconcile us back to that work and to the unified body of Christ.

We cannot serve people well when our spirits are broken and our bodies are exhausted. We cannot point people to the Third Way when our minds couldn't really care less. The work of leading toward oneness is exactly that: work. Just as fitness trainers advise us to take a day off between workouts so our muscles can recover, we need to recover our mental, physical, and emotional strength for the work of reconciliation too. Whether you're working toward oneness in a friendship, the way you think about yourself when you look in the mirror, your relationship with God, or your relationships with the people you consider your enemies, from time to time you've got to take a break. That's what family reunions are for. That's why we have girls' nights and date nights and porch sitting with our grandparents. No one can only and ever work on mending things without taking time to restore themselves to wholeness.

People who believe in the oneness that Jesus prayed for us are regular, ordinary people. We are not superhuman. We are not special. We are not exempt from anger, disappointment, sin, or frustration. We have our own prejudices and biases. We like some people better than others. It is critical that we remain aware of our preconceptions about others, as well as our weaknesses. Just the other day, I looked in my rearview mirror and saw a gentleman in the car behind me. Only, what I saw was not a gentleman. Without knowing anything about this man other than what I saw in my rearview mirror, I passed quick judgment on him. This, for me, is a clear indication that I've reached my limit and I need a break. Once I've recognized I've unfairly categorized another person, I know my next step is to confess my misstep to God and, when possible, another person. Then I need to take a break. I need to get away and leave the oneness work to someone else for a while, until my spirit, mind, and body have been brought back to their own sense of unity. I cannot bring oneness to my sphere of influence when I am broken down and worn out. Neither can you.

This is what is so fascinating about Jesus. He lived among us, fully divine and fully human. Yet he was without sin. By their very nature, divinity and humanity are like oil and water. They are opposites. Divinity is all about the supernatural, while humanity is wholly natural. Yet Jesus found a way to reconcile the two as he lived among us. Jesus was the perfect conduit to reconcile us to God. We aren't able to reconcile people to God. We aren't perfect as Jesus was. But we can work toward living in harmony with others. We can work toward introducing a paradigm shift, inviting others to seek unity over division. But making sure we are seeking oneness ourselves is a prerequisite.

Taking care of yourself is not selfish—it is essential. Even Jesus took time out to reconnect with the Father. How much more should we—who are fully human, although filled with the Spirit—be sure to do the same?

CONCLUSION

I believe each of us has a theme that runs through our lives. We look back over the times and seasons and realize our lives have been a series of chapters that continue one after another from childhood to old age, if we live long enough for that.

From a young age my interest has bent toward something I used to call diversity. That word, I now realize, is old, tired and, like all words, falls short of what it's supposed to mean. We co-opt words and define them according to our comfort zones. The words we use grow ineffectiveness around them. The meaning of words like *diversity, colorblindness, unity, tribe, multiculturalism, multiethnicity, tolerance, acceptance,* and others like these become diluted over time. It's difficult to talk about abstract concepts with any confidence the people in the conversation are on the same page.

Racism, prejudice, and *privilege* are words that have become compromised over time too. Depending on power structures, systems, and influence, different people get to hold more sway in saying which definition is the "right" one. What fits in one context offends in another. Even the idea of oneness can become distorted.

In the opening scene of the story God's been telling through the ages, God tells us that two shall become one flesh. Later, in Ephesians 5, Paul confessed the whole thing is a mystery. But then, Paul went on to say that the physical intimacy and commitment experienced by a married couple in love models the intimacy Christ desires us to have with the Father (see v. 32).

Author and rabbi Lawrence Kushner offers two beautiful metaphors (and, he insists, they are only metaphors) to help us think more clearly about this oneness with God. Before introducing the metaphors, Rabbi Lawrence said, "I'm going to say right up front that they are both just metaphors. Relax. Just metaphors." The rabbi knows our propensity for opening up or shutting down in response to the words we hear. Then, he continued, saying,

> The first way to describe our relationship with God is very familiar to many of us. In this understanding of how we relate to God, we often picture a big circle, and we imagine that circle represents God. Then, separate from the big circle, and below it, we imagine a tiny, little circle, and we imagine that circle represents me. You would imagine a very little circle of your own—separate from me, and below the big circle. That circle would represent you. In fact, in this model, each person is represented by a very little circle, outside of and below the big circle which represents God. This is the way many of us think about our relationship with God—tiny little circles, separated from each other and from God.
>
> The second metaphor, however, shifts our perspective just a bit. There is still a very big circle which represents God. In

this metaphor, however, the little circles that represent you and me are *inside* the big circle; not apart from it.[1]

When I heard Rabbi Kushner describe these two metaphors, I remembered something Jesus once said. Full of compassion for humanity, he said, "I have longed to gather your children together, as a hen gathers her chicks under her wings" (Matt. 23:37).

I have watched a mother hen gathering her chicks to herself. It was in Key West, Florida, on a city street between two parked cars, of all places. The mother hen spread herself out, puffing herself up and tucking the little ones beneath her body so that, if you didn't know better, you would find it hard to tell where the chicks end and the mother hen begins.

This is the oneness we've been talking about throughout this book. It is a shift in perspective that imagines us, not apart from God, but *in* God. Mysterious? Yes, to be sure. But it's a perspective that is consistent with the Word of God: "My prayer is not for them alone. I pray also for those who will believe in me through their message, that all of them may be one, Father, just as you are in me and I am in you. May they also be in us so that the world may believe that you have sent me" (John 17:20–21).

This is what it means to be one. We are so intimately connected—first to God and then to one another—that it becomes impossible to determine where one ends and the other begins. This was Jesus's prayer for us. Why? So the world will know that Jesus was sent by God.

Somehow, when I was a little girl, I noticed the way our churches divided themselves by race, and I knew in my heart that division was wrong. That understanding has never left me. Over the decades, I dreamed of a day when the Church could figure out a way to worship across racial lines, as a witness to the world of the power of the Holy Spirit. That dream has never gone away. Over the years, I've seen some individual churches that are living the dream. I've also seen individuals whose relationships with people are rich with diversity and the kind of oneness Jesus desires for us. These churches, communities, and individuals have embraced the vision of oneness—often without really trying too hard. If you've experienced these types of relationships or worshiped in these congregations, you understand the gifts God provides for us through his wildly creative cultures and personal journeys. You also know these kinds of experiences are far too often the exception to the rule.

The dream I have has been challenged and beaten down by people who tell me I'm foolish, misinformed, racist, ridiculous. I've had my setbacks. I've doubted that Jesus really came to tear down the wall that we build to keep one another at a distance (see Eph. 2:14–16). But the vision I see in my sanctified imagination is like one of those inflatable clown bop bags that, no matter how many times you knock it down, it rights itself again with its ridiculous smile and oversized eyes. I don't believe Jesus would pray for something that wasn't part of his Father's will for us. But we live in a reality where the kingdom of this world and the kingdom of God are battling for the same real estate.

From a worldly perspective, people do have legitimate reasons for why they choose to worship with some people and apart from others. Often people who live in America navigate systems of oppression on a daily, hourly, and moment-to-moment basis. Their guard is up at school, in the marketplace, in the workplace, in the play space. For many of these people, the local church is their weekly experience of furlough. Black men who are followed around in the department stores are trained to serve as ministry leaders in the black congregations. Black women who make significantly less than their white counterparts in the workplace are given responsibility for budgets and programs in their black churches. Latina sisters who feel pressured to abandon their first language simply because they live in America teach from the pulpits and Sunday school classrooms in their Spanish-speaking churches. Refugees from Burma who work as laborers in physically taxing environments are treated with the honor and respect they deserve in their Karen church services. Chinese immigrants who work in corporate America, paying careful attention to their diction and pronunciation, hear the Word taught to them in Mandarin each Sunday morning at church.

Our world discriminates against many. This is not the desire of God's heart. Often church is the only place for those not in the majority culture to be refueled for the week ahead. It's not only a matter of culture. It is a matter of spiritual, mental, and even physical survival. For those whose culture is not mainstream, church is often the only place where people know your story. Often their story is the same as your. When church works well, it consistently honors the *imago Dei* in a soul that is beaten down and treated with suspicion or disdain or impatience the other six days of the week. If this is true, while they may be a welcome refuge from an oppressive and exhausting culture, our segregated churches also stand as an indictment against the people of God to imagine and work toward the preferred future that Jesus's prayer invites us to embrace.

Our racial divisions aren't our only growing edges though. All of the ways we divide the body of Christ with regard to ideologies magnify the fact that we are only human. The more we embrace these concepts of oneness—passing through and celebrating one another's differences, practicing compassion, exercising grace, confessing as well as forgiving, desiring love over being right, lamenting and giving space for the lament of others, recognizing *all* life is holy, and all the other ideas we've discussed in these pages—the less division we will see in the Church. Trust me. Should the Church in America ever become the object of true persecution (there's a word we can restore to its original meaning), we will not be concerned about worship styles, doctrines, language, the role of women, and whatever other issue we have the luxury of dissecting today. We create these false, ungodly divisions because we have the luxury of doing so.

In the midst of true persecution, no one would be concerned with what *kind* of Christian any of us are. Instead, our false superiorities fall away when we realize what matters most. We would see that what matters is that all people are treated with love, respect, dignity, and honor. What matters is that we are actually our brothers' and sisters' keeper. When the Church begins to understand its role in making that happen in public life, our false and frivolous divisions begin to diminish. When the Church steps up and truly serves the least of these, we begin to embody the oneness Jesus prayed for us. We understand our connectedness to one another. We start to comprehend our position in Christ, rather than apart from him, and that understanding changes things.

Our divisions and categorizations and characterizations of one another are evidence of areas where we're missing the mark. This is why the experience of oneness—for those who have witnessed it firsthand—is so awe-inspiring. Like children witnessing Strandbeests walking on the beach, true oneness makes us forget that we ever imagined life any other way.

Like love, oneness cannot be forced or animated or treated as a project. People who are living it out should not lord their experience over anyone else's, because that will ultimately lead to more division. Oneness begins in the heart of each one of us. It edges out our doubts about its efficacy. It wears away our inhibitions. It instills in us a sense of hope. It expands our minds and enriches our imaginations. Oneness blurs the line we've drawn between ourselves and the rest of the world. Oneness, like love, transforms our affection for those we once called our enemy. Most important, like love, oneness does not call attention to itself. Love celebrates the object of our affection. Oneness, in the body of Christ, celebrates the power of the Holy Spirit at work in us and in the world, making all things new.

What a great opportunity we have before us. What a privilege to be on this journey, at this precise moment in time, along with you. We can step into the work of oneness and unity with confidence. Why? Because the same power that raised Jesus from the dead is alive in you and me. We are not fighting a losing battle. When we embrace the vision of oneness that Jesus prayed for us, we embrace the promise of good things to come. The Holy Spirit miraculously transforms us, and we mysteriously find ourselves looking at the world and the people in it in a new way.

For the sake of those watching how Christians engage with one another and with the world, let's get it right. This is our moment. We get to roll up our sleeves, here and now, and live out the ministry to which we've been called: showing Jesus to the world through our love for others. The odds are in our favor. God created us for this, Jesus prayed this for us, and the Holy Spirit empowers us to see it through.

We are more than conquerors, and we are in this together. It is an honor to work beside you, for such a time as this.

A NOTE FROM THE AUTHOR

Some dear friends of ours came to visit the other day. They were on their way to a family gathering in Colorado and spent the night with us to help break up the long stretch of car sitting and windshield gazing. We ate a meal together and talked well into the night, before sleep got the best of us. In the morning, Harry cooked eggs and bacon, and I rinsed off and dried some raspberries for our breakfast. After we ate, our friends packed up their belongings and we held hands together in the dining room, praying a blessing over one another and thanking God for his great provision of friendship.

Harry and I watched our friends drive away. These friends of ours are committed to unity and oneness in the body of Christ. We are fellow authors, and their stories have been instrumental in breaking down walls of division in the Church and in their communities. When we talk with them, our shared vision of unity and oneness keeps us close to one another. Our intimate knowledge of the struggles, the pushback, the success, and the grace of God in the midst of it all serves as an unbreakable tie that binds.

After our friends had driven out of sight, I went into the kitchen and turned on the television just in time to catch the early morning news reports of Alton Sterling being shot by law enforcement officers in Baton Rouge. Those who watched the video of the exchange between Alton and the police officers saw Alton die in front of their eyes. I didn't know it then, but I was watching the first of several violent events that would unfold over three consecutive days. This series of events brought the country to its knees, quite literally. The next day, Philando Castile died after being shot by a police officer in Minnesota during a traffic stop. Many of us watched his death live, as it was streamed online by Philando's fiancée, with her four-year-old daughter in the backseat of the car. And then, the next day, in a horrendous act, a sniper gunned down five law enforcement officers as they patrolled a peaceful protest, fulfilling their oath to serve and protect the city of Dallas, Texas.

On that first day, after our friends left our home, I spent a good portion of the day lying across the bed in our guest bedroom. I cried. I stared at the ceiling. I had a few conversations with God. Those conversations sounded like this: "What am I supposed to do? I have cried. I have prayed. I have spoken. I have written. I have protested. I have kept silent. And still . . . violence. What's up with that, God? What do I do now?"

I don't know that I was really expecting an answer. But I got one.

Late in the day I went out onto the deck to let myself get lost in the pages of a book I was reading. I hadn't been reading very long when two words seemed to stand out on the page:

"come together." I stared at those two words for a couple of moments.

How? I thought. *Where? Who? When?* Then, I thought to myself, *Never mind.* I mean, I'm just one person, right?

In the evening, my husband and I made a phone call to our son. We talked about the death of Alton Sterling, about what it meant and how we should respond. I told my son, "I don't know what to do. I have cried. I have prayed. I have spoken. I have written. I have protested. I have kept silent. And still . . ."

"Come together," my son said when my voice trailed off. And an idea began to take shape in my head. I remembered the promise that God will gather with us, whenever we come together, in his name.[1] God is not hindered by time or space, so the internet seemed the most likely gathering spot. The next day, working quickly, I put together a Facebook event, named it "Prayers of the People," and sent out invitations. We would pray together, for thirty minutes, from wherever we were in the world. The event was shared over and over again. Invitations were issued. By now we'd all learned about Philando Castile's death in Minnesota, and our hearts were broken yet again.

I thought maybe a dozen people or so would join in. But that afternoon at 4:00 p.m. (CST), more than four hundred people checked in to the event and joined in the praying. I wish I had words to describe it. Beautiful is a weak descriptor. Even holy seems to fall short. What I can tell you is that I am convinced that, through our unity, there is more power to impact the world for good than there is in our division.

The next day we learned of the tragic shooting in Dallas and joined for prayer again. Our time together was sweet and sacred, just like the previous day. The answer right there in front of us.

I don't know who in your life is difficult to love. I don't know the walls you've built or the lines you've drawn. Democrats? Republicans? Illegal immigrants? Terrorists? Gang members? White supremacists? Muslims? Law enforcement officers? Black Lives Matter supporters? LGBTQ community members? What I know for sure is that Jesus came to tear down all the walls we put up to keep one another at a distance.

Divisiveness and its tragic consequences are not unique to people living in the United States. People around the world have and do suffer oppression, marginalization, terror, and even death all because human beings allow small fissures in relationships with one another to grow into seemingly insurmountable walls of anger and hatred.

We have one true enemy, and it is not one another. If we get distracted from that, we do the enemy's work for him. If we look at other human beings, no matter how much we may disagree with them, and label them as "evil" or the "enemy," then we have missed the point. We have fallen into a trap. The only way out is beyond the walls. Across the lines. The only way to get there is by the power of the Holy Spirit in us. The only place to begin is on our faces, before God.

I wish there would never be another event like any of those our country experienced during that violent week in July 2016. But, remember, we are in the space between what is and what will be. In this life, we *will* have trouble (see John 16:33). It is for this reason we work out our salvation, right where we are. We don't get a free pass *out*, because we are salt and light *in* the world. Together, we are called to lift our voices in prayer *for* the terrorist, the shady politician, the protester, the criminal, the refugee, and the brokenhearted in our world, in our communities, in our churches, and beneath our roofs. God desires nothing less than that everyone know his great love for them—right here and now. He is counting on us to make it so.

The revolution begins in your heart. And in mine. May we be humble enough to let God transform us, beginning this very moment.

FOR ONE . . . OR MORE:
A STUDY GUIDE

This guide is offered as a tool to help you engage the content of each chapter of *One* at a deeper level. Feel free to use this guide as a personal study tool or as part of a small group study on oneness and unity. To engage in ongoing discussions around the themes presented in this book, join the conversation by visiting DeidraRiggs.com. There you can join the online book club "Forward" and search online archives for more information on oneness and unity.

Introduction

1. What did you learn about confrontation in your family of origin? How has that carried over to your feelings about confrontation today?

2. Are there individuals or groups of people who have offended you? How have you responded to the offenses?

3. Are you holding on to any regrets or grudges? What do you think it might take to release them? Why is this important?

Chapter 1: A Soul that Hears Well

1. What is the most essential aspect of your identity?
2. How have you been enlarged by people who are different from you? Write or talk about a specific experience.
3. What kinds of experiences and events make it difficult for you to love your neighbor well? Why?

Chapter 2: Integrated Experiences

1. Write or talk about your thoughts regarding divisions in the body of Christ. What divisions do you see? What divisions are just becoming clear to you?
2. In the Gospel accounts of Jesus's life and ministry, what do we learn about how Jesus responded to people who were different from him? How is your response to those who are not like you the same as Jesus's response? How is it different?
3. How is reconciliation defined in this chapter? Do you agree with that definition? What would you change? Why?
4. God instructed the Israelites to teach the commandments to the next generation and physically bind the commandments to themselves and to their homes. What practical steps can you take to teach the message of oneness to the next generation? How can you bind oneness and unity to your person and your home?

Chapter 3: What Do We Do about Evil and Injustice?

1. In your life, who are the people who have shown you the most grace? Write or talk about one of them. How did their expression of grace bring you closer to God?

2. Consider a person or group of people you do not understand, agree with, or like. Maybe you can revisit what you wrote in response to question 2 from the Introduction. What do you think might happen if you viewed this person or group of people from the mercy seat? Will you give it a try?

3. What does it mean to you when you hear that God is the God of both justice *and* mercy?

Chapter 4: Let It Go

1. What do you need to confess today? Write it down for your eyes only.

2. Where is God calling you to extend yourself across lines of division? What walls is God asking you to dismantle? Be specific in your answer.

3. What percentage of God's character do you fully comprehend? What is the most surprising thing God has revealed to you about himself?

Chapter 5: The Power to Unite

1. Complete these sentences, taken from chapter five:
   "Oneness is not about _____.
   Oneness is about _love & compassion_."

2. What do you think your younger self would say to you about how you're living out your faith today?

3. What is your desire for the people in this world who have hurt your feelings, oppressed your soul, discarded your body, or twisted your mind?

4. Satan is our one true enemy. Not people. People may set themselves up as our enemy, but we don't have to respond in kind. What happens when we mistake the actions of people *under the influence of evil* for the *evil one*?

Chapter 6: Awake in the Dark

1. How does it impact your view of God to know that he loves everyone, including Michael Brown *and* Officer Darren Wilson?

2. True or false: there is no right or wrong way to lament. Discuss your answer.

3. What are practical ways you've seen churches, cultures, and communities embrace and encourage lament?

4. To which do you feel drawn: prayer, protest, love, or lament?

Chapter 7: Our Breaking Point

1. When you think about your own experiences of broken-ness, have you felt more *broken open* or *broken apart*?

2. Spend some time today looking for evidence that we live in the overlap depicted in the illustration in chapter 7. Notice when you see evidence of the kingdom of God and when you see evidence of the kingdom of this world. Write

down what you notice. If you're working through these questions in a group, compare your lists with one another.

3. Spend some time in prayer. Ask God for wisdom about how to live as a citizen of the kingdom of God, here on Earth. Write down any thoughts that rise to the surface.

Chapter 8: Beyond Our Wildest Imagination

1. What kinds of things did you imagine when you were a child?

2. In what ways are you helping to shape culture in your everyday life?

3. When you allow your imagination to go wild, what kinds of dreams rise up in your soul? What might happen if you surrender your imagination to the Holy Spirit?

Chapter 9: One with Ourselves

1. Write a list of all the different roles you play in life. For example, you may be a child, a sibling, a spouse, an employer, and a volunteer. You may also be a caregiver, a Sunday school teacher, a Bible study leader, and a sculptor. Look at your list and begin to see them all as equally sacred in God's eyes. Invite God to remove any sacred/secular divide that might still exist in the way you approach your life.

2. Write a list of all the people who are *for* you. Say a prayer of blessing and thanksgiving for them.

3. For whom might you be willing to lay down your life?

Chapter 10: Return to Home

1. Write or talk about some of the most difficult experiences you've had while working toward oneness and unity.

2. How can you tell it's time for a break? What are the physical signs? What are the emotional and spiritual signs?

3. Describe the place you call home.

4. Make a plan to take a furlough or sabbatical for yourself. Mark the dates on your calendar.

Conclusion

1. Read John 17:20–23. Rewrite the prayer in your own words.

2. What does Jesus pray for in this prayer?

3. What does Jesus say will be the result?

ACKNOWLEDGMENTS

Thanks be to God the Father, Son, and Holy Spirit. You planted this concept in me when I was just two years old, and you have been growing it in me ever since. We are not done, Lord. You still have much to show me. Much to teach me. Thank you for the invitation to share, as best I can, your vision for us of oneness with you, oneness with ourselves, and oneness with others, even our enemies. I am a slow learner, Lord. Thank you for your mercy. I bless your name for all the ways I see this vision becoming reality. I thank you for redeeming us and always working to make all things new. I pray these words honor you.

To all my friends who prayed me through. You know who you are. Your prayers are woven through each page of this book.

Missy Scudder, I am quite sure this book would not have happened without your constant encouragement through emails and private messages. Your support has been a precious gift to me.

Katie Androski, Jane Rosenbaum, Amy Tilson—your stories and perspectives have helped shape my thoughts and words. Thank you for sharing so generously.

Thank you to my editor, Rebekah Guzman. Your calm and steady encouragement and your gentle guidance were pure gift.

Thank you, Amy Ballor, for pressing me to make sure the words on these pages make sense for the readers. I'm grateful for the collaboration.

Thank you to everyone who reads my writing online. For your comments, for asking the tough questions, for hanging in with one another. Thank you for being the most amazing practitioners of grace. Your love and support of one another gives me hope that oneness and unity are more than possible. I'll see you out there.

Thank you to my son, Jordan, who always promises, "It will be fine." And to my daughter, Alexandra, for giving this book a name. You are my favorites.

Thank you to Harry. For everything. I love you.

NOTES

Introduction

1. *Merriam-Webster's Collegiate Dictionary*, 11th ed., s.v. "confront."

Chapter 1 A Soul that Hears Well

1. David Brooks, *The Road to Character* (New York: Random House, 2015), 34.

2. Krista Tippett, *The Dignity of Difference*, audio podcast, October 29, 2015, http://www.onbeing.org/program/dignity-difference/188.

3. Terry Tempest Williams, "Engagement," *Orion*, July–August 2004, http://www.orionmagazine.org/article/engagement.

4. Brooks, *Road to Character*, 54.

5. William E. Pannell, *Working Together toward Racial Reconciliation*, accessed August 16, 2016, *FULLER*, https://fullermag.fuller.edu/working-together-toward-racial-reconciliation/.

6. Parker J. Palmer, "We Need to Find a Third Way," On Being, May 27, 2015, http://www.onbeing.org/blog/we-need-to-find-a-third-way/7611.

7. See Matthew 22:36–40.

8. Sarah Bessey, "Rethinking Scarcity: A Legacy of Abundance," The High Calling, June 22, 2014, http://www.thehighcalling.org/articles/essay/rethinking-scarcity-legacy-abundance.

9. John Blase, "That Next Place," The High Calling, April 5, 2015, http://www.thehighcalling.org/articles/essay/triptych-three-poems-easter.

Chapter 2 Integrated Experiences

1. "James Baldwin: How to Cool It," *Esquire*, April 29, 2015, http://www.esquire.com/news-politics/interviews/a23960/james-baldwin-cool-it/?src=social-email.

2. Martin Luther King Jr., "Remaining Awake through a Great Revolution," sermon, National Cathedral, Washington, DC, April 9, 1968, Martin Luther King Jr. and the Global Freedom Struggle, 11:16, http://kingencyclopedia.stanford .edu/encyclopedia/documentsentry/doc_remaining_awake_through_a _great_revolution.1.html.

3. "As Racial Hate Groups Rise, Strategies to Shut Them Down," PBS News-Hour, March 25, 2016, http://www.pbs.org/newshour/bb/as-racial-hate-groups -rise-strategies-to-shut-them-down/#transcript.

4. To learn more about cultural competency and its importance in this work for individuals and organizations, visit http://idiinventory.com.

5. Learn more about code switching at NPR's code switching site: http://www .npr.org/sections/codeswitch/2013/04/05/176352338/faq.

6. The Israelites were given 613 commandments (*mitzvot*) by God, to guide their daily interactions with him, with one another, and with other nations. These rules are recorded in the first five books of the Old Testament (also known as the Torah).

Chapter 3 What Do We Do about Evil and Injustice?

1. Immaculée Ilibagiza, *Left to Tell: Discovering God Amidst the Rwandan Holocaust* (Carlsbad, CA: Hay House, 2014), 204.

2. Ibid., 93–94.

3. Ibid., 210.

4. Desmond Tutu, *No Future without Forgiveness* (New York: Doubleday, 1999), 54–55.

5. Matthew Henry, *Micah*, Matthew Henry Commentary on the Whole Bible (Complete), http://www.blueletterbible.org/Comm/mhc/Mic/Mic_006 .cfm.

6. Bryan Stevenson, *Just Mercy* (New York: Random House, 2014), 290.

7. James Doty, *The Magic Shop of the Brain*, On Being, February 11, 2016, http://www.onbeing.org/program/james-doty-the-magic-shop-of-the-brain /transcript/8418.

Chapter 4 Let It Go

1. George Robertson, "We . . . and Our Fathers Have Sinned," First Presbyterian Augusta, June 26, 2015, http://firstpresaugusta.org/we-and-our-fathers -have-sinned-daniel-98/.

Chapter 5 The Power to Unite

1. Matthew 6:10.

2. "Who We Want to Become: Beyond the New Jim Crow," On Being, April 21, 2016, http://www.onbeing.org/program/michelle-alexander-who-we-want -to-become-beyond-the-new-jim-crow/transcript/8611.

3. Dian Land, "Study Shows Compassion Meditation Changes the Brain," University of Wisconsin–Madison, March 25, 2008, http://news.wisc.edu

/study-shows-compassion-meditation-changes-the-brain/#sthash.Ro7bYM
sU.dpuf.

4. Ibid.

Chapter 6 Awake in the Dark

1. United States Department of Justice Civil Rights Division, *Investigation of the Ferguson Police Department*, March 4, 2015, https://www.justice.gov/sites/default/files/opa/press-releases/attachments/2015/03/04/ferguson_police_department_report.pdf.

2. Olga Khazan, "Middle-Aged White Americans Are Dying of Despair," *The Atlantic*, November 4, 2015, http://www.theatlantic.com/health/archive/2015/11/boomers-deaths-pnas/413971/.

3. "Christians and Protest with Pastor and Activist Jonathan Brooks," *Quick to Listen*, March 2016, https://soundcloud.com/christianitytoday/christians-and-protest-with-pastor-and-activist-jonathan-brooks.

Chapter 7 Our Breaking Point

1. Parker J. Palmer, *Healing the Heart of Democracy* (San Francisco: Jossey-Bass, 2011), 149.

2. Stevenson, *Just Mercy*, 289.

3. "Top Civil Rights Lawyer Says US Criminal Justice Reforms Are Falling Short," PBS NewsHour, May 13, 2016, http://www.pbs.org/newshour/bb/top-civil-rights-lawyer-says-u-s-criminal-justice-reforms-are-falling-short/.

4. Stevenson, *Just Mercy*, 290.

5. Palmer, *Healing the Heart*, 18.

6. Stevenson, *Just Mercy*, 290.

Chapter 8 Beyond Our Wildest Imagination

1. Jamie Wax, "Artist's Intricate Creations Enjoy Long Walks on the Beach," CBS News video, 1:48, October 6, 2015, http://www.cbsnews.com/videos/artists-intricate-creations-enjoy-long-walks-on-beach/.

2. *Merriam-Webster's Online*, s.v. "culture," accessed September 19, 2016, http://www.merriam-webster.com/dictionary/culture.

Chapter 9 One with Ourselves

1. See 2 Corinthians 5:17.

2. Romans 7:24.

3. Martin Zwilling, "Lack of Integrity Is an Easy Quality to Detect," Business Insider, January 12, 2011, http://www.businessinsider.com/lack-of-integrity-is-an-easy-quality-to-detect-2011-1.

4. *13th*. Director Ava DuVernay. Netflix, 2016. Film.

5. See Luke 6:28.

Conclusion

1. "Transcript for Lawrence Kushner—Kabbalah and the Inner Life of God," On Being, March 10, 2016, http://www.onbeing.org/program/lawrence-kush ner-kabbalah-and-the-inner-life-of-god/transcript/8504.

A Note from the Author

1. See Matthew 18:20.

Deidra Riggs is a national speaker, author, and blogger. As founder of *JumpingTandem*, Deidra leads an online community offering inspiration, encouragement, and a safe place to practice grace. She is a regular contributor to Dayspring's (in)courage online community. She has been a speaker for TEDx, QWomen, and IF:Gathering. She has organized her own women's retreat and is founder and host of the ONE Conference (oneconf.us). She lives in Lincoln, Nebraska, with her husband, Harry, and their dog, Santana. Connect with Deidra at DeidraRiggs.com.

Also Available from DEIDRA RIGGS

Foreword by
Ann Voskamp

every

little

thing

Making a World of Difference
Right Where You Are

deidra riggs

In this encouraging and empowering book, Deidra Riggs calls you to accept God's invitation to join him in making a difference right where you are, right now.

Connect with DEIDRA!

DeidraRiggs.com

Learn more about Deidra's
Speaking • Writing • Events

@DeidraRiggs